Practical Concerns About Siblings:

Bridging the Research-Practice Gap

The *Journal of Children in Contemporary Society* series:

Practical Concerns About Siblings:

Bridging the Research-Practice Gap

Edited by
Frances Fuchs Schachter, PhD
Richard K. Stone, MD

SCHOOL OF PROFESSIONAL
CALIFORNIA
PSYCHOLOGY
LOS ANGELES

The Haworth Press
New York • London

Practical Concerns About Siblings: Bridging the Research-Practice Gap has also been published as *Journal of Children in Contemporary Society*, Volume 19, Numbers 3/4, Spring/Summer 1987.

The Haworth Press, Inc., 12 West 32 Street, New York, NY 10001
EUROSPAN/Haworth, 3 Henrietta Street, London WC2E 8LU England

LIBRARY OF CONGRESS
Library of Congress Cataloging-in-Publication Data

Practical concerns about siblings : bridging the research-practice gap/Frances Fuchs Schachter, Richard K. Stone, editors.
    p. cm.
    "Has also been published as Journal of children in contemporary society, volume 19, numbers 3/4, spring/summer 1987" — T.p. verso.
    Includes bibliographies and index.
    ISBN 0-86656-647-3
    1. Brothers and sisters. 2. Parent and child. 3. Sick children — Family relationships. I. Schachter, Frances Fuchs, 1930- . II. Stone, Richard K.
    [DNLM: 1. Sibling Relations. W1 JO584T v. 19 no. 3/4 / WS105.5.F2 P895]
  BF723.S43P73 1987
  155.4'43 — dc 19
  DNLM/DLC
  for Library of Congress   87-31095
                                                       CIP

Practical Concerns About Siblings:
Bridging the Research-Practice Gap

CONTENTS

ABOUT THE EDITORS

Frances Fuchs Schachter is Associate Professor of Pediatrics at New York Medical College and Supervising Pediatric Psychologist at Metropolitan Hospital Center, New York. She is in private practice in Riverdale, the Bronx, New York. Professor Schachter was formerly Chief Psychologist at St. Luke's Hospital, New York, and Supervising Psychologist at Columbia Presbyterian Hospital. She has served on the faculty of Stanford University, Bank Street College of Education, and Barnard College, Columbia University.

Richard K. Stone is Professor of Clinical Pediatrics at New York Medical College and Chief of Pediatrics, Metropolitan Hospital Center, New York.

Practical Concerns About Siblings:

Bridging the Research-Practice Gap

Foreword

Why this volume? And why now? Its title suggests a gap between what researchers think about siblings and what therapists, educators, social policy makers, and parents are actually *doing* in the realm of siblings. "Gap" is possibly an understatement about the existing gulf between what happens in the trenches and what happens in the laboratory of the social scientist. This gulf flows two ways. Researchers, to make their work relevant and vital, must let themselves be influenced by the common sense and experience of people who work in the real lives of families. Likewise, practitioners should base some of their interventions upon a solid foundation of evidence, informed by good research.

The people who contributed to this landmark collection work in diverse settings from the busy wards of urban hospitals to the quiet halls of academe. Some specialize in the everyday problems of ordinary families; others specialize in the problems of families in difficult situations. Yet, whatever their perspective, the writers address the pains, paradoxes, and complexities of the sibling drama in a most practical way.

In the small New England town where I live and work, an announcement appeared recently in the local paper:

> THE SIBLING EXPERIENCE. Learn to help your
> child cope with the birth of the new baby.

The class, taught by a nurse, has become a regular and well-attended part of the prepared (Lamaze) childbirth program. Obviously, "siblings" is an idea whose time has officially come. This volume will have gone a long way if it can help the teachers of such seminars, not to mention policy makers, psychotherapists and parents themselves. It's a long way from the researcher's report to the actual practice of improving peoples' lives. This volume shortens the distance.

Stephen P. Bank, PhD
Wesleyan University

Preface

Research on siblings is almost as old as the science of psychology itself. The first studies were conducted 100 years ago in the British laboratory of Darwin's cousin, Sir Francis Galton. Yet, sibling research has just begun to address the many practical concerns of families and of professionals working with families. Earlier work focused on static variables such as the age-gap between siblings or the order of their birth, factors that proved to play a minor role, if any, in the emotional and social development of children. In the last decade, a growing interest in the family, in family therapy, in the changing family, and in the family as the focus of preventive health care, has prompted researchers to investigate dynamic processes and problems in sibling relationships.

Indeed, in recent years, there has been an outpouring of research on sibling relationships as never before and the work proceeds with apace. Improved methods and new theories have been applied to research on common sibling problems such as coping with the new sibling. At the same time, increased attention has been paid to the concerns of children in special sibling relationships such as those with dying siblings. The time seems ripe for an edition disseminating these findings and discussing their implication for parents and for providers of human services to children and their families. Hence this volume.

In selecting the papers for this volume, we aimed to be comprehensive, and to review contemporary research on sibling relationships in all its variety. We also aimed to keep pace with current developments; some of the findings are published here for the first time. Finally, we tried to bridge the gap between research and practice by minimizing professional jargon and by providing case material and practical suggestions.

xiii

The first section of the volume reviews research on common sibling problems, coping with the new sibling, sibling conflicts, comparing and contrasting siblings, and favoritism. The second section covers the concerns of children in special sibling relationships, children in one-parent families, siblings of the mentally ill, children with a disabled sibling, and finally those facing the imminent death of a sibling. The last section addresses the question: Can siblings be part of the solution rather than part of the problem?

The volume should prove valuable to a broad range of professionals working with children and families, including social workers, pediatricians, nurses, psychologists, family therapists, other therapists, psychiatrists, teachers and their students. Researchers should also welcome this volume as a compendium of current work on siblings. Parents too should find the volume useful; it will help them distinguish between fact and fiction in the advice offered by parent manuals.

We would like to thank Linda Smalls-Spence and Maxine Daughtry for their help in preparing this volume.

Frances Fuchs Schachter, PhD
Richard K. Stone, MD

Introduction

Judy Dunn, PhD

The sibling relationship is one of distinctive emotional power, passion and intimacy, of competitiveness, and of emotional understanding that can be used both to provoke and to support. To parents and to clinicians, and now belatedly to developmental psychologists, it is a relationship of great significance and interest, one that contributes to the harmony or disharmony of the family and to the pattern of individual children's development within the family. For parents, the nature of the relationships between siblings is a matter of much importance. The qualities of emotional power, competition and lack of inhibition that characterize the relationship can mean that conflict between siblings is both common and often violently expressed (Strauss, Gelles & Steinmetz, 1980). Aggression between siblings is deeply upsetting to parents as they are shocked by it and bewildered about how to stop it (Newson & Newson, 1968). For clinicians and educators concerned with the care of children, a difficult sibling relationship is often seen as not solely symptomatic of adjustment problems but as contributing to them. Practitioners are frequently faced with practical decisions that involve siblings: Should they be kept together at all costs? Are the siblings of handicapped children or those with serious illnesses at risk for problems and how can they be helped? Can siblings act as support for one another in families in which the parents have serious problems? Is the relationship inevitably one of conflict and rivalry?

In the face of these urgent needs and practical concerns, what

Judy Dunn is Professor of Human Development, The Pennsylvania State University, College of Human Development, Henderson Building, University Park, PA 16802.

can researchers offer in the way of help? How far and in what ways do the results of systematic research help the stressed parent or the clinician faced with a troubled family? More generally, does research on siblings help us to understand the pattern of relationships within a family? And how can researchers learn from parents and practitioners who deal with siblings in difficulty? The "bridge" that needs to be built between research and practice is two-way. But how near are we to finding such a bridge?

The papers in this volume give us some encouraging answers. The editors are to be congratulated on bringing together these papers, making available to practitioners, parents and researchers such useful material, with such good timing. Until relatively recently, research into social-emotional development in childhood focused almost exclusively upon the relationship between mother and child. Whether it was research aimed at answering questions about clinical problems or at tracing normal developmental patterns, it was the relationship of mothers with their children that was seen as the all-important social influence. While many clinicians felt that we should attempt to understand how *family* patterns of relationships contribute to disturbance in children, systematic research focused exclusively upon mothers. Mother and child were studied as a dyad isolated from the other relationships within the family and from the broader social context.

Over the last decade, however, it has been increasingly and widely recognized by developmental and clinical psychologists that children grow up within a network of family relationships, relationships that influence one another in complex ways and that change over time (see for instance the special issue of *Child Development* edited by Kaye and Furstenburg [1985]). It is clear that if we are to understand how children develop in the ways that they do, we must systematically study these complex and dynamic patterns of influence within the family. Research into siblings has clearly shown the importance of these family patterns. From this research, we can learn not only useful practical lessons about the problems faced by parents and about the ways in which those in the caring professions can help troubled children, but we can learn lessons about how and why children develop as individuals, about the origins of individual differences. These three themes run through the chapters in this book: first, the problems (and pleasures) of bringing up siblings within the family and what we can do to help parents; second, the special problems experienced and presented by siblings facing particular stresses and the clinical lessons to be learned from recent research; and third, the understanding of normal developmental principles that we gain from studying siblings.

Common to all three themes, and of major significance to each, are two issues. The first is the significance of individual differences between children and between sibling dyads. The second is the close interlocking of the relationships between siblings and parents, especially the significance of differential treatment by parents. As we read through the papers, we see the significance of these two issues, their importance to a practical grasp on how to deal with problems, and their importance to a deeper understanding of individual development and emotional adjustment in childhood.

COMMON PROBLEMS

The first two papers deal with what are probably the main parental concerns about siblings. First, Vandell summarizes the findings of research on the effects of the arrival of a sibling. It is clear that the impact of a sibling's birth, at least for firstborn children, is a major one. Children show their distress and disturbance at this upheaval in their lives in a variety of ways. The documentation of their disturbed behavior will not surprise clinicians; such disturbance is familiar to them. The recent research, however, does begin to make it possible for us to understand which children are most vulnerable to this event and why, to understand which features of the situation are most stressful, and to suggest some practical ways in which parents can help their children. The individual differences in children's responses to the birth of a sibling are notable, and research shows us which children are likely to be particularly upset, and how to reduce the stress that they experience.

There are in fact some surprises for the clinician or parent in the research findings. Three unexpected results that are important for parents to know are the following: first, the results show that the *age* of the firstborn at the time of the sibling birth is relatively unimportant in contributing to the extent of disturbance children show as compared with the significance of differences in children's personalities or in their relationship with their parents; second, the results show that breast-feeding the second born does not appear to be a source of trauma to the firstborn (as is suggested in several parent manuals); and third, the findings from longitudinal studies show that an initial reaction of anger and difficult behavior does not imply that a poor relationship between the siblings will develop. In contrast, a reaction of withdrawal by the firstborn child *is* associated with a poor sibling relationship later on, and it should be a matter of concern to the practitioner (Dunn & Kendrick, 1982). There are clear and useful messages for families, in the results of this research, messages that are important in a situation that is often very difficult for both firstborn and for parents.

What researchers should learn from parents is also important. In our own study of the arrival of a sibling, parents gave us a number of important leads: insights that had clear practical significance, and observations that had important developmental implications. One insight was that many firstborn children found the changes in daily routines accompanying the birth of a sibling to be particularly disturbing. The practical implication was clear: parents should try to minimize the changes in their children's routine at the time of the sibling birth. An instance of a strikingly important observation was the finding that many children made important developmental *advances* at the time of the sibling's birth, a result confirmed in later studies.

While quarrels between siblings are hardly a major issue for parents in the first few months after a sibling's birth, they *are* a dominating issue through the next 16 or so years when the siblings are home together. Brody and Stoneman discuss this issue, such a central one for parents, in their chapter. Their answer to the question "What makes siblings quarrel?" emphasizes both individual differences in siblings' temperament, and patterns of family management of the sibling relationship. It is an answer that brings us directly to the issue that recurs again and again throughout the book: the significance of parental differential treatment of their children, and the interlocking of parent and sibling relationships. Brody and Stoneman's advice for parents, based on their own research, stresses the importance of equal treatment of siblings within the family, and of nonintervention in sibling conflict. These two points stand out again in Bryant and Litman's chapter which emphasizes the value of parents' "distancing" themselves from the siblings' relationship. They show us how complex the interconnections of sibling-child and parent-child relationships can be. Their research findings imply that if both parent-child and sibling-child relationships are punitive, or both are nurturant, they have important and deleterious effects on the children. It is, they argue, most helpful if the two relationships are balanced or complement each other rather than if each reinforces the other.

For the practitioner, Bryant and Litman's paper clearly defines the implications of research into these interconnections between relationships within the family. They discuss, for instance, how the sibling relationships can be a real help for children in families in which parents are "unavailable." They also point out that an extremely strong sibling bond may indicate problems in the parent-child relationship, and they emphasize that it is wise not to separate siblings at times when the parental relationship is under stress. They spell out how useful siblings may be as therapists, but emphasize that the sibling relationship is part of a family system, and thus the effectiveness of siblings as therapists will differ according to the parental cultural values. They also provide helpful pointers for distinguishing siblings who are functioning normally from those who are in need of help.

That conflict between siblings is *normal* and can indeed contribute to the important process of self-definition is a central theme in Schachter and Stone's paper. Schachter's previous reports suggest that siblings develop different or contrasting identities in order to mitigate everyday sibling rivalry and conflict, a phenomenon that she calls "sibling deidentification." In this volume, Schachter and Stone stress that parental intervention within the "normal" processes of conflict resolution and reconciliation between siblings can lead to problems. They describe a pattern that they term "pathological deidentification" in which one sibling is assigned the identity of "angel-victim," and the other is seen as the "devil" who is always harassing the angel, and parents constantly intervene to protect the angel. Clinical strategies to treat such a pattern are suggested.

The consensus of these chapters is, then, that parents should "stay out" of sibling conflict, and they should distance themselves from the sibling relationship. My cautious reaction, as a researcher and as a parent, is that we should be concerned here about *cause* and *consequence*. It is not surprising that if siblings do not get along well together, the family atmosphere is conflict-ridden and parents repeatedly attempt to mediate between their children or to stop them from arguing. We need yet more careful research, however, to be clear about the "direction of effects," about which is cause and which is consequence. The great value of these chapters is that they set out clear hypotheses about the direction of effects that further research can test, and they do make clear practical suggestions.

Bank suggests that differential parental treatment may entail yet other risks for a child in addition to the problems of a difficult sibling relationship. He explores the origins of an extreme case of favoritism, which he sees as centered in the parent's own traumatic childhood, and argues that while to be a favorite may seem life-saving to a child, it carries the risk of a child being too closely involved in and subjected to a parent's emotional problems. The extremes of favoritism and rejection that he describes are relatively rare in the general population, but Bank, in the psychoanalytic tradition, uses a clinical history of an extreme case to help us understand the commonplace. To discover whether this clinical strategy bears fruit, and whether such extremes are indeed attributable to transgenerational effects will require research that takes into careful account the differences in children within the family, the parents' current state, and the family circumstances. We should take note of Bank's emphasis on the urgent need for such research and the lessons for researchers implicit in his clinical case history.

SPECIAL CONCERNS

In the second section of the book, the papers that discuss siblings in single-parent families, children with handicapped siblings, and siblings with life-threatening illness not only give us very important practical information based on careful research, but they lead us to question some commonly held beliefs. Shapiro and Wallace give us an encouraging picture of the sibling relationships within single-parent families, and of the strengths in the one-parent family. The same themes that arise in discussing siblings in two-parent families arise here, but they are heightened in emphasis in the tighter-knit relationships of the one-parent family. Thus the themes of the *ambivalence* in siblings relationships (i.e., emotional mix of support and comfort with conflict and quarrels), the complexity of the interconnections between the different relationships, and the individual differences in how children respond to stress, clear in the research on the impact of a sibling birth, are again strongly emphasized in this paper. It will be important to repeat such research on samples larger than the 13 families whom Shapiro and Wallace studied, but equally important to replicate their study without losing the sensitivity of their multi-interview methods, which gives us a vivid picture of each family member's perception of the family relationships.

In families with disabled brothers and sisters, the significance of parental differential treatment for the adjustment of the nonhandicapped sibling is again evident. McHale and Gamble's chapter shows with clarity how research on families with special problems can not only give practical advice but can illuminate issues of general developmental importance. The lessons from their own research into the siblings of disabled children are many. They draw attention, for instance, to the significance of the children's interpretation of their disabled sibling's behavior (surely important with nonhandicapped siblings too), and of the children's perceptions of what happens between them. There are not, for example, more sibling problems reported by children with disabled siblings than by children with nondisabled siblings. Yet, the children with disabled siblings *perceive* their problems as more troublesome to them. McHale and Gamble's results lead us to question some of the usual assumptions about families with disabled children. They show, for instance, that children's satisfaction with their relationships with disabled siblings is not related to measures of their emotional well-being, that it is not time spent caregiving a disabled sibling per se that leads to problems for the nonhandicapped siblings; rather, it is the extent of conflict with the disabled sibling, and whether they feel that they are treated fairly by the parents relative to their disabled sibling. Their paper highlights, as did the earlier papers discussing families with nonhandicapped siblings, the importance of individual characteristics of the child, of the sibling, and of the family context, but shows us how the importance of these characteristics differs for families faced with the challenge of coping with a disabled child.

The impact of a stressful experience upon very young children is brought almost unbearably close to us in Sourkes' chapter on the siblings of cancer patients. It is an overwhelmingly poignant account. Our attention is drawn to the strengths of the relationship for both children, to the importance of seeing the relationship as two-way, and again to the issues of the complexity of the connections between parent-child and sibling-child relationships. As with the children of single-parent families, the importance of these links between parent- and sibling-child relationships appears even more heightened than within families not facing such stresses. Sourkes gives many important practical recommendations for helping these children, suggestions that are sensibly and sensitively justified, and set in the context of quotations that vividly illustrate the children's pains and needs. As just one illustration, the point made by McHale and Gamble on the significance of the children's perceptions or understanding of the other's behavior is echoed again when Sourkes shows us how crucial it is to understand the children's version of the cause of the sibling's disease if effective intervention is to be provided.

DEVELOPMENTAL IMPLICATIONS

The practical insights to be gained from these chapters are clear, and helpful. In addition, the discussions bring to light a number of important developmental principles, relevant to both normal and special populations. In Rowe and Elam's paper, this is particularly striking. They start from the observation that within families there may be patterns of resemblance between family members, but there are also striking differences. Siblings, for example, who share the same family environment and also 50% of their segregating genes, nevertheless grow up to be markedly different from one another in personality, in problem behavior, and in adjustment. Rowe and Elam take the example of behavior problems to illustrate a profoundly important developmental theme: that if we examine the sources of influence on individuals within a family and separate out those influences (genetic and environmental) that are shared or common to the siblings from those influences (genetic and environmental) that affect one but not another sibling, we find that it is the nonshared environmental influences that are of major importance in contributing to the development of individual differences (Plomin & Daniels, 1987). This point is especially well illustrated by studies of siblings, especially of adoptive siblings, who are brought up together with the same parents, the same family atmosphere, and the same environmental advantages or disadvantages, yet who differ markedly in adjustment and personality.

The demonstration of the significance of nonshared environmental influences has revolutionized the way in which we think about early environmental influence. What are the sources of these different and formative experiences for children within the same family? Rowe and Elam spell out the different possibilities, one of which is that siblings themselves directly affect each other, but in different ways. Schachter's notion of deidentification is clearly central here. Another possibility is the theme that has recurred so often in the book: that differential treatment by parents has long-term and important effects on developmental outcome. The implications of the research on siblings is, as Rowe and Elam show, of central importance in our understanding of why people develop in the ways that they do. Rowe and Elam have specific suggestions about how clinicians can help researchers to gather the information we need to understand more clearly how far each of the possible sources of nonshared environmental influence contributes to the development of individual differences.

A second general developmental theme that is illustrated in the sibling research is the complexity of the balance between different social influences within the world in which children grow up. It is a theme that, as we have noted, is echoed in many of the chapters, and it is particularly clearly stated in Bryant and Litman's discussion on the connections between parental and sibling roles. Their chapter highlights, too, a third theme: that of the specific influence of one sibling upon another through teaching. Here their discussion shows how such teaching *may* happen and in experimental settings does indeed happen. We still need to know how far such teaching does occur in the real world and how extensive its effects are. To answer that question, more naturalistic studies are needed.

It is clear from naturalistic studies of sibling quarrels, play and conversation that even if teaching is relatively rare between siblings, many of their daily exchanges are particularly powerful *learning* contexts for the domain of social understanding. Children confronting their siblings over clashes of interest, for example, demonstrate remarkably sophisticated powers of understanding the other, of social rules, and of how these can be used to one's own advantage (Dunn, 1987; Dunn & Munn, 1985). The importance of developing the ability to resolve conflict and to negotiate reconciliation is emphasized, as we have seen, by Schachter and Stone and by Bryant and Litman among others. Our own studies show that the less conciliatory aspects of conflict may also be developmentally valuable, perhaps an encouraging note for parents tired of the endless arguments between their children. In parallel fashion, within the context of a friendly affectionate sibling relationship, children show remarkably early the ability to take part in joint pretend play. As young as 24 months, children can enact, explore, and exploit social roles within the context of a shared nonliteral framework, a remarkable intellectual achievement for such young children (Dunn & Dale, 1984).

Naturalistic studies could help us also to understand the processes involved in a fourth developmental theme that the sibling research highlights: the influences on children's developing sense of identity and their sense of self. The part that siblings play in influencing children's sense of identity is most explicitly set out in Schachter's "deidentification" theory. What we need now is research that will enable us to assess the extent of such influence and the ways in which it is executed.

The practical and theoretical lessons and insights that these papers give us are, then, many. Most encouraging of all, they show us that careful systematic study of siblings as family members can be, and is being conducted in spite of the complexity of the enterprise. It is within the family that children grow and develop. If we are to understand the origins of their problems and their happiness, and how we can best help and support them, then it is within the family world that we must study them. The research in these papers begins to show us the way.

REFERENCES

Dunn, J. & Kendrick, C. (1982). *Siblings: Love, envy and understanding.* Cambridge, MA: Harvard University Press.

Dunn, J. & Dale, N. (1984). I a Daddy: 2-year olds' collaboration in joint pretend with sibling and with mother. In I. Bretherton (Ed.), *Symbolic play: The development of social understanding*, pp. 131-158. New York: Academic Press.

Dunn, J. & Munn, P. (1985). Becoming a family member: Family conflict and the development of social understanding in the second year. *Child Development, 56,* 480-492.

Kaye, K. & Furstenberg, F. (Eds.) (1985). *Child Development, 56,* No. 2.

Newson, J. & Newson, E. (1968). *Four years old in an urban community.* London: Allen and Unwin.

Plomin, R. & Daniels, D. (1987). Why are children within the family so different from each other? *The Brain and Behavioral Sciences, 10,*1-16.

Straus, M. A., Gelles, R., & Steinmetz, S. (1980). *Behind closed doors.* New York: Doubleday.

PART I:
COMMON PROBLEMS

Baby Sister/Baby Brother:
Reactions to the Birth of a Sibling
and Patterns of Early Sibling Relations

Deborah Lowe Vandell, PhD

SUMMARY. The birth of a sibling is a major event in a child's life. This paper discusses common reactions to the birth of a sibling, characteristics of early sibling relationships, and factors affecting children's initial reactions to the birth, and the children's developing interactions with their siblings. Evidence of stability over time in the quality of early sibling relations is also examined. The implications for parents of these studies on early sibling relations are discussed.

The birth of a sibling is a major event in a child's life. In the United States, it is typically preceded by the mother leaving the child for several days. When the mother returns, she is accompa-

This paper was written while the author was a visiting scholar with the New England Node of the MacArthur Foundation Network Studying the Transition from Infancy to Early Childhood. Requests for reprints should be sent to the author at Program in Psychology, University of Texas at Dallas, Richardson, TX 75080.

nied by a little creature who takes up an incredible amount of her time and energy. And, this creature doesn't go away. Instead, over time, it becomes more and more a presence as it crawls, walks, and then runs headlong into the older child's life. It seems inevitable that this sibling will have a profound impact on the older child. In this paper, some of the effects of the sibling birth on the older children will be explored. It will also examine the nature of children's developing relationship with their infant sibling. Because the reaction to the new sibling and the early sibling relationships can vary widely, a variety of factors affecting these reactions will be outlined. These factors include the nature of the children's relationships with their mothers, degree of paternal involvement with the children, individual temperamental differences, and the children's age at the birth.

IMMEDIATE REACTIONS TO THE BIRTH OF THE SIBLING

Although some children appear to be only minimally affected (Dunn & Kendrick, 1982; Legg, Sherrick & Wadland, 1974; Nadelman & Begun, 1982; Thomas, Birch, Chess & Robbins, 1961), many children have pronounced physical and psychological reactions to a sibling's birth. Indeed, Winnicott (1964) has claimed that negative reactions to the birth of a sibling are so pervasive as to be viewed as "normal."

Interviews with mothers about their children's reactions support the contention of widespread effects. Trause, Voos, Rudd, Klaus, Kennell, and Boslett (1981), for example, interviewed mothers prior to their second children's births and again shortly after discharge from the hospital. Ninety-two percent of the mothers reported an increase in behavioral problems in their children following the sibling's births. Fifty-four percent of the mothers reported increases in behavioral problems in three or more areas. Areas highlighted included sleeping problems, temper tantrums, and excessive activity. Thomas et al. (1961) found very similar reactions in their large scale study of temperament; 18 families experienced a sibling birth during their project. Over half of these children were reported to regress socially, to have feeding, sleeping, and toilet training problems.

Legg, Sherrick, and Wadland (1974) studied a range of reactions to the birth of a sibling in children between 11 1/2 months and 5 years. Consistent with other reports, many children showed regression in toilet training, feeding, and sleeping as well as increased attention-getting behavior. Legg et al. (1974) also noted increased aggressiveness directed towards the mother. It was only after the new siblings were mobile and able to get into the older children's things that aggression was typically directed towards the younger siblings.

Nadelman and Begun (1982) had mothers report their first born children's reactions to the younger sibling's birth via an open ended questionnaire and a standardized rating scheme. When they contrasted maternal reports one month before and one month after the birth, they found a number of negative changes in the children's behaviors. The older siblings were reported to be less easy to talk to, less alert, and fussier about going to bed. They also seemed to be having greater difficulty getting along with peers.

Dunn and Kendrick (1982), and Dunn, Kendrick, and MacNamee (1981) have provided one of the most detailed and extensive analyses of the effects of the birth of a sibling on older children's behavior. Forty English working class families were interviewed prior to the birth of a second child and again one month after the birth. As in the other studies, many children had pronounced reactions to the birth. Ninety-three percent of the mothers reported an increase in their older children's being naughty and demanding. Regressive behaviors were reported for 70% of the children. Sleeping problems increased in 28%. Toilet training difficulties occurred in almost half of the children who had been trained prior to the baby's birth. Dunn and Kendrick (1982) also noted problems in the children's relationships with other family members. About 50% of the mothers reported the children were jealous when they saw the baby with either the father or the grandparents. Although aggression was rarely directed at the baby, mothers noted the older child would try deliberately to irritate the baby by putting their faces too close or taking away a toy the baby was interested in.

These studies then appear to document widespread disruptions in children's behaviors following the sibling's birth. It should be remembered, however, that these reports were based on maternal interviews. Consequently, they are subject to the criticism that the mothers were biased in their reports. Their own fatigue and physical discomfort could have made the mothers more demanding and critical of their older children. Certainly, many mothers report that they are very tired and depressed following the birth of the second child (Dunn & Kendrick, 1982), and to outside observers the mothers appear to be extremely fatigued (Taylor & Kogan, 1973).

In addition, mothers' perceptions and interpretations may be colored by their own reactions to the new baby. Young, Bayle, and Colletti (1983) have noted that some mothers reacted to the impending and actual birth with sadness, guilt, and anger over the way that necessitated changes in their relationships with their first borns. These mothers were unhappy about being able to spend less time with the older child, and they felt guilty about depriving the older child of their time together. Young et al. (1983) observed that these mothers, as a consequence, were over-solicitous and over-indulgent towards the older children. They further suggested that the mothers' ambivalence over the new babies may have interfered with the mothers' ability to cope with their older children.

Direct observations, however, suggest that children's reactions to the sibling's birth are not strictly an artifact of maternal perceptions. In a carefully controlled set of observations, Field and Reite (1984) observed preschoolers' activity levels, sleep patterns, and interactions with a parent before and after the sibling's birth. Sleep disturbances were observed in 13 of the 16 children. Activity level was heightened 2 days after the birth while the mother was still at the hospital but depressed 10 days later after the mother had returned home. Field and Reite (1984) argued this pattern was consistent with heightened arousal associated with the short-term separation from the mother followed by a sense of helplessness and depression when the mother and the new sibling came home.

Other marked changes also appeared. The children's fantasy play increased after the birth, with 11 of the 16 children reflecting themes of aggression against the sibling and/or mother. And, the children's interactions with their mothers changed. Amount of time in cooperative play decreased and both mother and child were less responsive to the other's suggestions of play themes.

Dunn and Kendrick (1980, 1982) also observed mother-child interactions before and after the birth of the sibling. Following the birth of the sibling, periods of joint play decreased markedly and mothers were less likely to initiate interactions with their older children. The mothers' helping, showing, and cuddling their first borns decreased by almost one-quarter. At the same time, confrontations between mother and child increased dramatically. Not surprisingly, these conflicts often occurred when the mother was involved with the baby. Children were three times as likely to do something deliberately naughty when their mothers were with the babies. One child, for example, systematically dribbled milk from her cup onto the sofa while her mother was feeding the baby. Changes were also found in the mothers' conversations with the older children. Following the birth of the sibling, mothers used a higher proportion of prohibitions and their conversations dealt more with issues of control.

Others (Taylor & Kogan, 1973; Trause et al., 1981) have also noted pervasive changes in the quality of mother-child interaction with the birth of the sibling. Trause et al. (1981) found in home observations 1 to 2 weeks after the birth that mothers increased the number of angry, stern commands to their older children. At the same time, the children were clingier and stayed closer to their mothers than before the birth. Taylor and Kogan (1973) found both mother and child were less warm towards one another following the birth and there was evidence of less contingent turntaking after the sibling's birth.

Fortunately, the negative reactions to the birth of a sibling are often complemented by signs of positive growth and development. Consistent with Anna Freud's (1965) observation that periods of stress and apparent regression can also be periods of growth and progression, children may have positive reactions to the sibling's birth. Dunn and Kendrick (1982) noted some positive feeling towards the birth and positive changes in the older children's behavior. Fully 95% of their sample were reportedly eager to care for the baby. Eighty percent talked about the baby, and 75% tried to cuddle or caress the baby. In addition, over half of the children showed evidence of increased maturity and independence such as starting to go to the toilet unassisted or trying to dress themselves. Legg et al. (1974) and Nadelman and Begun (1982) also recorded enhanced development following the birth. Children were better able to play independently and separated more easily from their mothers. Others relinquished their pacifiers. Trause et al. (1981) reported that the older sibling's eating improved.

EARLY SIBLING RELATIONSHIPS

Thus far in this chapter, we have been describing children's initial reactions to the birth of a sibling. We have seen that for many children the birth is at least a short-term stress. Parents believe that this stress is outweighed by the children's benefit from having siblings. They have hopes that their children will develop special relationships with each other that are warm and supportive. They often anticipate that having a sibling will facilitate the development of empathy and social understanding and keep their children from becoming too self-centered. At the same time, parents may harbor fears that their children's relationships with one another will be marked by unbridled aggression and conflict.

In this section, we will examine the growing literature which describes early sibling interactions and relationships. Factors associated with positive, supportive interactions and conflicted, aggressive interactions will be outlined. Finally, because the enduring quality of these early relationships is an important question, issues of consistency or stability over time will be examined.

Sibling Caretaking and Teaching

Anthropologists (Barry & Paxson, 1971; Weisner & Gallimore, 1977) have documented the widespread incidence in different cultures of older siblings serving as caregivers for their younger brothers and sisters. Although young siblings are less likely to have major child care responsibilities in the United States than in some other cultures (Whiting & Whiting, 1975), there is still evidence that young American siblings sometimes function in caregiving ways.

In a series of studies, Stewart (1983a; Stewart & Marvin, 1984) examined whether preschool-aged siblings would take care of their infant siblings. Infants and their older siblings were observed in a modified Ainsworth strange situation (a laboratory procedure involving a series of separations and reunions from the mother and the preschool-aged sibling). All the infants cried when the mother left them in the laboratory playroom. Over half of the preschool siblings then responded to their younger siblings' distress by trying to comfort them. The children used a variety of strategies including hugging the infant, verbally reassuring the infant, carrying the infant, and trying to distract the infant with toys.

In a follow-up study, Stewart and Marvin (1984) tried to determine why some children responded to their siblings' cries and other children turned away. They hypothesized that part of the explanation was related to the children's understanding of the situation and their siblings' needs. When Stewart and Marvin (1984) compared preschoolers who were able to take the perspective of another person on a conceptual problem-solving test with preschoolers who could not take the other's perspective, they found the perspective takers were more likely to comfort their younger siblings.

This ability to take the perspective of the other person was also related to another set of sibling behaviors, namely sibling teaching. In an additional study, Stewart (1983b) asked preschoolers to teach their younger siblings how to operate a toy camera. Some preschoolers were very involved and effective in working with their younger brothers and sisters while others were less effective. Consistent with his observations of sibling caregiving, Stewart found those siblings who were better perspective takers on a test of social cognition were more active and thorough teachers.

Siblings as Attachment Figures

Recent studies (Dunn & Kendrick, 1982; Samuals, 1980; Stewart, 1983a) also suggest that young siblings can serve as attachment figures. As noted by attachment theorists (e.g., Ainsworth, 1973), children's emotional attachment to significant others can act as a source of security. This attachment relationship is marked by a balance between exploration and proximity seeking. When the infant is frightened or uncomfortable, s/he seeks proximity with the attachment figure. When the child feels safe and secure, s/he moves away from the attachment figure and begins to explore.

Stewart's work (1983a) on sibling caretaking showed that some infants used their older siblings as attachment figures. In these families, when a stranger entered the laboratory playroom, the infants would appear uneasy and move closer to their older sibling. They would then position themselves so that the older child acted as a barrier to the stranger. From this protected position, the infants would start to engage the stranger in interaction.

Samuals (1980) also found evidence of infants' attachment to their older siblings. Consistent with the notion that the presence of an attachment figure should facilitate exploration, she found that toddlers were more likely to explore an unfamiliar backyard when their older sibling was present than when the older sibling was absent.

Attachment can also be signaled by missing the attachment figures when they are not available. Fifty percent of the mothers in an English sample (Dunn & Kendrick, 1982) reported that their 14-month olds missed their older siblings when they were absent.

Siblings as Antagonists

A prevailing concern for some parents and clinicians is the incidence and intensity of sibling conflicts and aggression. In fact, most young siblings fight. In one set of home observations of toddlers with their preschool-aged siblings, fully 29% of the children's initiation/response exchanges were hostile (Abramovitch, Corter & Lando, 1979). The older children typically initiated these conflicts and the younger children usually submitted to the older children's aggression. In those rarer instances in which the younger siblings initiated the aggression, the older children would then counterattack.

Dunn and Kendrick (1982; Kendrick & Dunn, 1983) also noted the incidence of aggression and fights between young siblings. Half of the mothers they interviewed reported fights to occur at least daily between 14-month olds and their older siblings. Within that group, three-fourths of the mothers reported extreme hostility between the children. Kendrick and Dunn (1983) also observed that the older children initially took the lead in the aggressive encounters with the younger children deferring to the older siblings. With age, however, the younger siblings become increasingly aggressive.

At the same time, there is a striking range of individual differences in the frequency of aggressive encounters. During Dunn and Kendrick's (1982) home observations, one pair never fought, while 100% of another pair's interactions were antagonistic. Later in this chapter we will examine factors associated with these individual differences.

Siblings as Rivals

Burlingham and Freud (1944) have emphasized the rivalry for parental attention and affection which can occur between siblings. Observations indicate this desire for parental attention is often apparent in young siblings. In some of the first systematic observations of early sibling interaction, Lamb (1978a; 1978b) contrasted the social behaviors of preschoolers and their toddler siblings towards one another and their parents. He found one notable similarity in the siblings' behavior. Both children seemed to prefer interacting with their parents rather than with one another.

Dunn and Kendrick (1982) have other evidence of early efforts to secure parental attention. They found many 14-month olds tried to push their older siblings out of the way when the older children were being cuddled by their mothers or fathers. Similarly, the most common response of the older siblings to their mothers playing with the 14-month olds was to protest and demand the same attention. Rivalry was less apparent when the mother was involved in caregiving or disciplining the younger child. The majority of the mothers also reported that their children "minded" if the father played with the other child.

It is interesting that this rivalry is not necessarily the result of the mothers treating the children differentially. Several researchers (Corter, Abramovitch & Pepler, 1983; Dunn, Plomin & Nettles, 1985; Jacobs & Moss, 1976) have documented underlying similarities in many mothers' treatment of their children. Each of these studies have found positive correlations in mothers' behaviors towards their offspring.

Siblings as Playmates

In addition to fights and quarrels, young siblings also play with one another. This play takes several forms: imitative sequences including some games, prosocial exchanges, and, as the children get older, pretend play. Imitation between siblings is common. In their home observations of toddlers and their preschool-aged siblings, Abramovitch, Corter, and Lando (1979) noted that 20% of the siblings' initiations/responses involved imitation. Dunn and Kendrick (1982) also recorded a surprisingly high incidence of imitation. Ninety-three percent of the older siblings imitated their newborn siblings. When the younger siblings were 14 months, 86% of the older siblings were reported to imitate their toddler siblings; and 89% of the toddlers imitated their older siblings. Relationships were found over time between the siblings' imitation. When the older child imitated the younger more at 8 months, the younger imitated the older more at 14 months; and these imitative sequences seem to play an important role in the quality of the developing sibling relationship. Those siblings who imitated one another more also had more affectionate and friendly relationships with one another (Dunn & Kendrick, 1982).

If the work on toddlers' earliest games with peers is any indication (Ross, Goldman & Hay, 1979), the earliest sibling games probably involve imitation. My own children, Ashley and Colin, had a well organized imitative game which began when Ashley was 4 months. The game would start when Ashley would look at Colin and squeal. Colin would then look at Ashley and squeal back. These squealing exchanges were then typically repeated through at least 5 complete rounds. On occasion, 5-year-old Colin would start the game by looking at Ashley and squealing. Ashley would then copy Colin's squeal and the game would proceed. Both appeared to enjoy the game immensely: they would smile broadly and Ashley would flap her arms with each squeal in this game which was played daily during this period.

More systematic observations reveal the importance of games for somewhat older siblings. Sixty-seven percent of the mothers in the Dunn and Kendrick study (1982) reported that their toddlers and preschoolers played games such as hide and seek, peekaboo, and chase together daily. These games were part of a larger configuration of behaviors. Those older children who frequently played games with their younger siblings were more likely to help care for their younger siblings. Both children were also relatively more likely to imitate the other.

As the younger siblings reach the end of the second year, some sibling pairs begin collaborating in pretend play (Dunn & Dale, 1984). In this play, 2-year olds start to assume a pretend identity in a pretend place, transformations which are exceedingly complex for such young children. Not all young siblings engage in fantasy play together, however. Those children who share their fantasy play also have warmer and friendlier relationships with one another (Dunn, 1985).

Prosocial Concerns

The birth of a sibling greatly increases the opportunity for young children to consider the needs and wants of others. When mothers' conversations with their children prior to the sibling's birth are examined, it seems that mothers typically talked about these children's wants and needs (Dunn & Kendrick, 1982). After the birth of the sibling, however, references to others' needs (in particular the new sibling's) greatly increase. Dunn and Kendrick (1982) found 60% of the references by the children and their mothers to the needs of other people now refer to the younger sibling.

There are numerous examples in the literature of siblings behaving in a prosocial way towards one another. In his observations of preschoolers with their toddler siblings, Lamb (1978a, 1978b) noted that preschoolers would sometimes offer toys to their younger sibs. Abramovitch, et al. (1979) also observed that a substantial proportion of the initiations between toddlers and their preschool-aged siblings were prosocial acts such as sharing objects, providing help, comfort and physical affection. While these prosocial initiations were typically performed by the older sibling, the younger siblings directed fully 35% of the prosocial initiations.

Siblings as Communication Partners

In addition to playing, fighting, sharing, and helping, young siblings "talk" to one another. Some researchers have begun to document the forms of early sibling communication. These studies have been heavily influenced by earlier observations of mother-child communications (Snow, 1977) which show mothers modify their speech to their infants and toddlers in systematic ways. When they speak to their young children, mothers use a simpler vocabulary, frequent repetitions, higher pitch, attention getting devices such as "hey!" and shorter sentences. These linguistic forms are believed to be an effective way of eliciting attention and responses from infants as well as an ideal form for teaching language to children. One of the questions asked about early sibling interaction is whether young siblings are also effective communication partners.

Preschool-aged siblings do make speech modifications when talking to their younger siblings (Dunn & Kendrick, 1982; Tomasello & Mannle, 1985). Dunn and Kendrick (1982) found that even 2 1/2-year olds dramatically changed their speech when talking to their infant sibs. In fact, the children's speech to the infants contained an even higher proportion of repetitions and attention getting devices than did the mothers' speech to the infants. The older children's speech forms were also indicative of the quality of the siblings' relationship. Friendly interactions were more frequent when the older siblings asked questions and used diminutives with the younger children than when the older children never used these forms.

At the same time, critical distinctions between the older siblings' and mothers' speech were noted. The mothers used a much higher proportion of questions which were seen as reflecting the mothers' interest in understanding the babies' needs and the mothers' desire to construct turntaking "conversations" with the babies. The older siblings' utterances to their siblings, on the other hand, were often attempts to prohibit, dissuade, restrain, or direct.

Tomasello and Mannle (1985) also found important distinctions between children's conversations with their siblings and their mothers. They videotaped toddlers with their older siblings and mothers on two occasions between 12 and 24 months. The preschoolers were much less likely than their mothers to talk to the toddlers. The children also used a higher proportion of directives and fewer questions; and the preschoolers appeared less sensitive than the mothers to the toddlers' interests. Mothers were more likely to follow the toddlers' attentional focus or to acknowledge the toddlers' utterances. After the initial initiation/ response, there were fewer joint interactions between siblings than between mothers and toddlers.

Similar differences in mother-child and sibling communication are apparent in even younger pairs. When Vandell and Wilson (1986) contrasted the structure of turntaking exchanges between siblings and between mothers and infants at 6 and 9 months, they found infants spent much more time in turntaking exchanges with their mothers. Differences were also found in the forms of these interactions. Mothers were more likely to create long turntaking exchanges by responding contingently to their infants' nonsocial activities and then eliciting further infant responses around those activities. The preschoolers were unlikely to build an exchange around the infants' interests (unless they were taking away a toy the infants were interested in). Instead, the preschoolers would typically elicit brief responses from the infants around activities that the older children wanted the infants to do.

Ambivalent and Mismatched Relationships

Although some have described sibling relationships as a continuum ranging from positive/loving to hostile/negative (Einstein & Moss, 1967), siblings can incorporate both positive and negative aspects into their relationships. Dunn and Kendrick (1982) have distinguished between three separate patterns of early sibling relationships. Some children had very positive relationships in which they played games together regularly and the elder child helped with the baby. These siblings would often imitate one another. Other siblings had almost exclusively negative relationships. They fought most of the time and appeared to delight in their sibling's distress. At the same time, many young siblings combined positive and negative components into a pattern of ambivalence. Thus, some siblings who had intense fights also comforted one another. Some who seemed concerned when their younger siblings were reprimanded also directed negative behaviors towards the siblings.

Other sibling relationships involved a mismatch between the children (Dunn & Kendrick, 1982). While most younger siblings reacted positively to their older siblings, older siblings were more likely to react negatively to their younger brothers and sisters (Abramovitch et al., 1979, 1980; Lamb, 1978a; Dunn & Kendrick, 1982). This meant, then, that some sibling pairs were giving different messages and were thereby creating different sibling environments for one another.

FACTORS INFLUENCING THE INITIAL REACTIONS TO THE NEW SIBLING AND THE QUALITY OF EARLY SIBLING INTERACTIONS

Thus far, we have examined differences in children's reactions to their new siblings and different patterns of relationships between these siblings. In this section, factors associated with positive and negative reactions to the birth of the sibling and the developing sibling relationship will be detailed. Some of these factors may be useful to parents and health care professionals who are interested in minimizing adverse reactions to the sibling birth and fostering positive sibling relationships. Other factors may be less amenable to outside efforts, although parents may still derive some comfort in knowing that their situations are shared by other young families.

Quality of the Children's Relationships with Their Mothers

There are suggestions in the clinical literature (Levy, 1934; Legg et al., 1974) that children who are especially close to their mothers prior to the sibling's birth may have more negative reactions than do children with less close relationships with their mothers. The argument is that these children may feel most displaced by the new baby. Recently, Dunn and Kendrick (1982) have noted a different initial reaction. They found more negative initial reactions to the birth in those families in which there had been a high degree of confrontation and conflict between mother and older child before the birth. Confrontations, conflict, and prohibitions increased more markedly in these families in the first month postpartum than in other families. These results suggest that children with more positive relationships with their mothers prior to the birth may be better able to sustain the initial stress of having a new sibling in the house.

At the same time, Dunn and Kendrick (1982) have other data suggesting that, at least for girls, a very close relationship between mother and daughter can negatively impact the developing sibling relationship. In those families in which there was a higher frequency of joint play and attention between mother and daughter before and immediately after the birth, both siblings were less friendly to one another at 14 months. Similarly, very close relationships between the mothers and second children appeared to bode poorly for sibling relationships. When mothers had very warm and positive interactions with the younger sibling, both children were subsequently more hostile towards the other. In contrast, in those families in which there was a high level of conflict, prohibitions, and spankings prior to and immediately after the birth, girls (but not boys) were friendlier to their younger sibling at 14 months.

While these observations may have implications for parenting strategies, they should be interpreted with caution. First, I do not think that they suggest parents should have poorer relationships with their children so the children can have better relationships with their siblings. While siblings can serve as substitute sources of love and affection when mothers are especially hostile, the long-term effects of this substitution have not been studied. It may be better to have a loving relationship with a sibling than to have no positive, supportive familial relationships, but the negative effects of maternal rejection are probably not offset by sibling affection.

A second observation of note is that siblings had more negative relationships when their mothers were very close to one of the children. It may well be that jealousy and rivalry are intensified in those cases when the mother is especially close to one child at the expense of the other child. In order to minimize these negative reactions, mothers may want to insure that one child does not receive a disproportionate share of her attention. In the period after the birth of the second child, for example, mothers may want to minimize the sharp drop in their interaction with and attention to the first child. If the father and others can help in the care of the second child, the mother may be freer to ease the transition for the first child. As the children get older, mothers should be sensitive to the importance of balancing the children's needs.

In a more positive vein of fostering positive relationships between the siblings, positive sibling relationships appear to develop in those families in which the mothers talked to the children about their siblings as people with their own wants and needs (Dunn & Kendrick, 1982). These conversations apparently facilitated the growth of social understanding between the children and fostered positive interactions between the children.

Mothers' reactions to their children's conflicts can also be important. There is some support for Ginott's (1969) contention that the ways mothers handle their children's quarrels can systematically intensify or defuse their children's altercations. Relationships have been found, for example, between mothers' reactions to their sons' quarrels and the children's subsequent likelihood to quarrel (Kendrick & Dunn, 1983). In those families in which mothers responded negatively to the boys' quarrels with the babies at 8 months, the children became subsequently more quarrelsome at 14 months.

The Mother's Involvement with the New Baby

Following the birth of the siblings, most older children's interactions with their mothers now occur in the context of the mothers' interactions with the babies. Mothers are more likely to interact with their first borns when they are also with the babies (Dunn and Kendrick, 1980, 1982). Maternal involvement with the new babies elicits a variety of positive and negative responses from the older children. On the one hand, children are more likely to have positive interactions with their mothers when the mothers are holding or feeding the babies than when the mothers are not involved with the babies (primarily because the mothers are much less attentive to the older children when they are not with their babies). At the same time, children apparently do not like the mother to be with the baby. Acts of deliberate naughtiness are significantly greater at that time.

Extent of Paternal Involvement

One offshoot of the birth of the new child is that many fathers become increasingly involved with the older children (Dunn & Kendrick, 1982; Legg et al., 1974). While fathers may be only minimally involved with the new baby, they often take a more active role in the care of the older children. Positive benefits appear to be associated with this heightened paternal involvement. Conflicts between mother and the older child were less when the father was more involved (Dunn & Kendrick, 1982). Also, joint play between mother and child were greater when paternal involvement was greater. Finally, negative reactions were minimized when the fathers were more involved with the older children both prior to and after the birth of the sibling (Legg et al., 1974).

Child Temperament

Children's temperamental dispositions affect reactions to the siblings' birth and the siblings' subsequent relationships (Dunn, Kendrick & MacNamee, 1981; Legg et al., 1974; Thomas & Chess, 1977). Children who were extremely negative in mood prior to the birth of the sibling were more likely to be withdrawn and to have sleeping problems after the birth (Dunn, Kendrick & MacNamee, 1981). Those children who were characterized by extreme emotional intensity and negative moods were "clingier" after the birth. Children who were more withdrawn prior to the birth showed less positive interest in the new sibling. Those children who were characterized by mild, positive, regular responses and who readily adapted to new situations prior to the birth of a sibling showed this same pattern of responses to their new siblings (Thomas & Chess, 1977).

Age of the Older Child

There is considerable evidence that younger children have more pronounced negative reactions to the birth of a new sibling (Henchie, 1963; Legg et al., 1974; Robertson & Robertson, 1971; Trause et al., 1981). Both Trause et al. (1981) and Legg et al. (1974) found the greatest difficulties occurred when the older sibling was less than 18 months at the birth. Similarly, Dunn et al. (1981) found, in their comparisons of the reactions of children between 18 and 43 months, that younger children were "clingier" than older children following the birth. The Robertsons (1971) also reported that children under two years had a harder time adjusting to the siblings' birth than those children over 2 1/2 years, while Henchie (1963) found overt negative reactions occurred in 89% of the children who were under 3 years of age and in only 11% of the children who were over 6 years. Nadelman and Begun (1982) found more pronounced negative reactions in children under 40 months as opposed to those over 40 months. Immature behaviors, apathy, and frustration/aggression showed sharper increases in those children who were younger than 40 months. Nadelman and Begun also found some evidence that young boys were most affected by the sibling's birth.

In parallel to the decrease in negative reactions in older children, there is evidence that older children may welcome the new sibling. Children who were older than 4 1/2 or 5 years seemed very interested in the baby and wanted to hold it and care for it, while younger children were less positively inclined (Legg et al., 1974).

Initial Reactions to the New Sibling

Some parents are concerned about the first encounter of their older children with the new sibling. The hope/fear (depending on the initial reaction) is that this meeting may set the stage for subsequent encounters. No long-term effects have been found, however, between children's first reactions to the new sibling and the children's longer-term psychological or physiological responses or the siblings' subsequent relationships with one another (Dunn & Kendrick, 1982; Trause et al., 1981). Some children whose initial reactions were positive later decided they wanted to "send the baby back." Likewise, some children who initially responded negatively developed positive relations with their siblings while others continued their negative response. As will be outlined later in this chapter, however, there does appear to be some consistency in the quality of sibling relationships after the first few weeks.

Breast versus Bottle Feeding

Spock (1969) has suggested that confrontations and conflicts related to the new sibling are more likely when mothers breast feed the new baby. Legg et al. (1974) provide some support for this position. They found children reacted negatively to the mothers' breast feeding. Whenever the mother was nursing the baby, the older siblings would also want to nurse, or want the mother to play with them, or want to be held by the mother. The older children appeared to be actively vying for maternal attention.

Dunn and Kendrick (1982; Kendrick & Dunn, 1980), on the other hand, found no significant increases in confrontation or deliberate naughtiness in children whose mothers were breast feeding. In fact, they observed more joint play and less confrontation during breast feedings than bottle feedings. They link their observations to two factors. In their study, mothers who were breast feeding were more likely than mothers who were bottle feeding to make arrangements for their older children before beginning the feeding. The mothers tried to minimize potential conflicts by setting out activities for the older child, getting drinks of water, etc. prior to the feeding. Dunn and Kendrick (1982) also found indications that breast feeding mothers had closer relations with their first children. When the mothers were not with the baby, they spend more time playing with the older child. Also, prior to the birth, they were more likely to hold and to talk to the older child.

Hospital Visits

There are indications that visiting the mother in the hospital (when the mother feels strong enough) can have at least short-term benefits for the children and their mothers. All of the mothers interviewed by Legg et al. (1974) reported that hospital visits eased their children's distress at being separated from mother. Trause et al. (1981) also found some benefits to hospital visits. When children's reactions during the discharge from the hospital were compared, they found children who had not visited their mothers were more likely to ignore or avoid their mothers' requests for a hug or kiss. The nonvisitors were also more likely to ignore or respond negatively to parental comments and questions about the new baby. Fortunately, this avoidance was not longlasting. When the children were observed in their homes 1-2 weeks later, no differences were found in those who had visited their mothers and those who had not. Given these results, then, it appears that visits may help children's adjustment temporarily, but not in any longer-term way.

Preparation for the Sibling

Legg et al. (1974) have outlined a number of other factors which either facilitated or hindered children's adjustment to the new siblings. They found children responded more negatively to the birth (a) when they were cared for by an unfamiliar person or in an unfamiliar place during the mother's absence, (b) when they did not know ahead of time who would be caring for them in their mothers' absence, (c) when the family moved to a new house shortly before or after the birth, (d) when the children's sleeping arrangements were modified shortly before or after the birth by giving the babies the older children's cribs or rooms, and (e) when the children's schedules and routines were interrupted. Because of these observations, Legg et al. recommended minimizing changes and surprises occurring in the older children's lives around the time of their siblings' birth.

Multiple Siblings

Because most studies (Dunn & Kendrick, 1982; Taylor & Kogan, 1974; Trause et al., 1981; Field & Reite, 1985) examining reactions to the birth of a sibling have focused on first born children's reactions to the second child, we know little about the reactions to new siblings in larger families. Legg et al., (1974), however, have suggested that latter born children's reactions to subsequent siblings may be less pronounced. More research is clearly needed in this area before expectations and advice are solidified.

STABILITY IN THE QUALITY OF EARLY SIBLING RELATIONS

Part of the reason for examining the quality of early sibling interactions is the implicit concern that the quality of these early relationships is enduring. There are indications of at least moderate stability over time in the quality of early sibling relations. Vandell (1981) found consistency in the older siblings' interest in and activities with their younger siblings at 6 and 9 months; and Lamb (1978b) found a similar stability when the younger siblings were 12 and 18 months. Those children who were more likely to hit and to struggle for toys with their 12-month-old siblings were also more likely to hit and struggle for toys when those siblings were 18 months old. Those older siblings who were more likely to smile, vocalize, laugh, and share with their siblings at 12 months were more likely to display these behaviors with the 18-month olds as well.

Abramovitch, Corter, Pepler, and Stanhope (1986) have evidence of stability in the quality of sibling interactions over even longer periods. They observed siblings when the younger child was 20 months, 38 months, and 60 months. Although they found little stability over time in the frequencies of specific acts directed to the siblings, they did note stability over time in the overall affective tone of the siblings' relationships. Those siblings who displayed a higher proportion of positive to negative behaviors at 20 months also had a higher proportion of positive behaviors at 38 months. Those with a higher proportion of positive behaviors at 38 months then had a more positive affective tone in their relationships at 5 years.

Dunn and Kendrick (1982) also found moderate associations between reactions to the infant sibling at 2-3 weeks postpartum and the siblings' interactions at 8 and 14 months. Those children who had friendlier reactions to their infant sibling at 2-3 weeks were more likely to have friendly interactions at 14 months. Early imitation of the infant sibling was also associated with more positive interactions 14 months later. Consistency was also apparent in friendly interactions between 8 and 14 months. Finally, those children who had unfriendly interactions with one another at 8 months were more likely to be unfriendly at 14 months as well.

Dunn (1985) has additional evidence of the stable quality of early sibling relations in a longitudinal follow-up of her sample conducted by Stillwell (1984). Stillwell (1984) observed the children when the first born siblings were 6 years old. She found that positive warm sibling relationships in the 6-year olds were predicted by warm and friendly sibling interactions 3 years earlier.

CONCLUSIONS

I began this paper by proposing that the birth of the sibling is a major event in the young child's life. From the studies reviewed, it is clear that children have a variety of reactions to a sibling birth which includes disruptions in their physical and psychological functioning as well as apparent growth in these same areas. Moreover, the significance of the new sibling does not stop at the birth. In the weeks and months after the birth, the young children begin to develop their relationships with one another. Research shows that early sibling interactions incorporate a number of activities including helping, teaching, sharing, fighting, and playing; and that young siblings can act as emotional supports, rivals, and communication partners. While the relationships of some young siblings are predominantly positive, others are negative or ambivalent in nature.

In this paper, we explored how reactions to the sibling's birth and the relationship between the siblings were influenced by a variety of factors including the children's relationships with their mothers and fathers, the children's temperaments, and the children's ages at the births. Finally, it is important to note that the quality of these early sibling relationships is moderately stable during the preschool years. An important issue yet to be explored is whether the quality of sibling relationships is stable over even longer periods.

REFERENCES

Abramovitch, R., Corter, C. & Lando, B. (1979). Sibling interaction in the home. *Child Development, 50*, 997-1003.

Abramovitch, R., Corter, C. & Pepler, D. (1980). Observations of mixed-sex sibling dyads. *Child Development, 51*, 1268-1271.

Abramovitch, R., Corter, C., Pepler, D. & Stanhope, L. (1986). Sibling and peer interaction: A final follow-up and a comparison. *Child Development, 57*, 217-229.

Ainsworth, M. D. S. (1973). The development of infant mother attachment. In B. M. Caldwell & H. N. Ricciuti (Eds.), *Review of Child Development Research* (Vol. 3). Chicago: University of Chicago Press.

Barry, H. & Paxson, L. M. (1971). Infancy and early childhood: Cross-cultural codes 2. *Ethnology, 10*, 466-508.

Burlingham, D. & Freud, A. (1944). *Infants without families*. London: Allen and Unwin.

Corter, C., Abramovitch, R. & Pepler, D. J. (1983). The role of the mother in sibling interaction. *Child Development, 53*, 1599-1605.

Dunn, J. (1985). *Sisters and Brothers*. Cambridge, Mass.: Harvard University Press.

Dunn, J. & Dale, N. (1984). I a daddy: Two-year-olds collaboration in their pretend play with sibling and mother. In I. Bretherton (Ed.), *Symbolic play: The development of social understanding*. New York: Academic Press.

Dunn, J. & Kendrick, C. (1980). The arrival of a sibling: Changes in the patterns of interaction between mother and first-born child. *Journal of Child Psychology and Psychiatry, 21*, 119-132.

Dunn, J. & Kendrick, C. (1981a). Interactions between young siblings: Associations with the interaction between mother and first born. *Developmental Psychology, 17*, 336-344.

Dunn, J. & Kendrick, C. (1981b). Social behavior of young siblings in the family context: Differences between same sex and different sex dyads. *Child Development, 52*, 1265-1273.

Dunn, J. & Kendrick, C. (1982). *Siblings: Love, envy and understanding*. Cambridge, Mass.: Harvard University Press.

Dunn, J., Kendrick, C. & MacNamee, R. (1981). The reaction of first-born children to the birth of a sibling: Mothers' reports. *Journal of Child Psychology and Psychiatry, 22*, 1-18.

Dunn, J. F., Plomin, R. & Nettles, M. (1985). Consistency of mothers' behaviors toward infant siblings. *Developmental Psychology, 21*, 1188-1195.

Einstein, G. & Moss, M. S. (1967). Some thoughts on sibling relationships. *Social Case Work, 48*, 549-555.

Field, T. & Reite, M. (1984). Children's responses to separation from mother during the birth of another child. *Child Development, 55,* 1308-1316.

Freud, A. (1965). *Normality and Pathology in Childhood.* New York: International Universities Press.

Ginott, H. G. (1969). *Between parent and child.* New York: Avon Books.

Henchie, V. (1963). *Children's reactions to the birth of a new baby.* Unpublished master's thesis. Institute of Education, University of London.

Jacobs, B. S. & Moss, H. A. (1976). Birth order and sex of sibling as determinants of mother-infant interaction. *Child Development, 47,* 315-322.

Kendrick, C. & Dunn, J. (1980). Caring for a second baby: Effects on the interaction between mothers and first-born. *Developmental Psychology, 16,* 303-311.

Kendrick, C. & Dunn, J. (1983). Sibling quarrels and maternal responses. *Developmental Psychology, 19,* 62-70.

Kreppner, K., Paulsen, S. & Schuetze, Y. (1982). Infant and family development: From triads to tetrads. *Human Development, 25,* 373-391.

Lamb, M. (1978a). Interactions between eighteen-month-olds and their preschool-aged siblings. *Child Development, 49,* 51-59.

Lamb, B. (1978b). The development of sibling relationships in infancy: A short term longitudinal study. *Child Development, 49,* 1189-1196.

Legg, C., Sherrick, I. & Wadland, W. (1974). Reactions of preschool children to the birth of a sibling. *Child Psychiatry and Human Development, 5,* 3-39.

Levy, D. M. (1934). Rivalry between children of the same family. *Child Study, 11,* 233-261.

Nadelman, L. & Begun, A. (1982). The effect of the newborn on the older sibling: Mothers' questionnaires. In M. E. Lamb & B. Sutton-Smith (Eds.), *Sibling relationships: Their nature and significance across the lifespan.* Hillsdale, N.J.: Erlbaum.

Robertson, J. & Robertson, J. (1971). Young children in brief separations: A fresh look. *Psychoanalytic Study of the Child, 26,* 264-315.

Ross, H. S., Goldman, B. D. & Hay, D. F. (1979). Features and functions of infant games. In B. Sutton-Smith (Ed.), *Play and learning.* New York: Gardner Press.

Samuals, H. R. (1980). The effect of an older sibling on infant locomotor exploration of a new environment. *Child Development, 51,* 607-609.

Snow, C. E. (1977). The development of conversation between mothers and babies. *Journal of Child Language, 4,* 1-22.

Spock, B. (1969). *Baby and child care.* New York: Pocket Books.

Stewart, R. B., Jr. (1983a). Sibling attachment relationships: Child-infant interactions in the strange situation. *Developmental Psychology, 19,* 192-199.

Stewart, R. B., Jr. (1983b). Sibling interaction: The role of the older child as a teacher for the younger. *Merrill Palmer Quarterly, 29,* 47-68.

Stewart, R. B., Jr. & Marvin, R. S. (1984). Sibling relations: The role of conceptual perspective taking in the ontogeny of sibling caregiving. *Child Development, 55,* 1322-1332.

Stillwell, R. (1984). *Social relationships in primary school children as seen by children, mothers and teachers.* Unpublished doctoral dissertation, University of Cambridge, England.

Taylor, M. K. & Kogan, K. L. (1973). Effects of birth of a sibling on mother-child interaction. *Child Psychiatry and Human Development, 4,* 53-58.

Thomas, A., Birch, H. G., Chess, S. & Robbins. (1961). Individuality in responses of children to similar environmental situations. *American Journal of Psychiatry, 117,* 798-803.

Thomas, A. & Chess, S. (1977). *Temperament and development*. New York: Brunner-Mazel.

Tomasello, M. & Mannle, S. (1985). Pragmatics of sibling speech to one-year-olds. *Child Development, 56,* 911-917.

Trause, M. A., Voos, D., Rudd, C., Klaus, M., Kennell, J. & Boslett, M. (1981). Separation for childbirth: The effect on the sibling. *Child Psychiatry and Human Development, 12,* 32-39.

Vandell, D. L. (1981). *Encounters between infants and their preschool-aged siblings during the first year.* Paper presented at the biennial meetings of the Society for Research in Child Development, Boston, Mass.

Vandell, D. L. & Wilson, K. S. (1986). *Infants' interactions with mothers, siblings and peers: Contrasts and inter-relations.* Manuscript submitted for publication.

Weisner, T. S. & Gallimore, R. (1977). My brother's keeper: Child and sibling caretaking. *Current Anthropology, 18,* 169-190.

Whiting, B. B. & Whiting, J. (1975). *Children of six cultures: A psychocultural analysis.* Cambridge, Mass.: Harvard University Press.

Winnicott, D. W. (1964). *The child, the family, and the outside world.* London: Penguin Books.

Young, P. C., Bayle, K. & Colletti, R. B. (1983). Maternal reaction to the birth of a second child: Another side of sibling rivalry. *Child Psychiatry and Human Development, 14,* 43-48.

Sibling Conflict:
Contributions of the
Siblings Themselves,
the Parent-Sibling Relationship,
and the Broader Family System

Gene H. Brody, PhD
Zolinda Stoneman, PhD

SUMMARY. To understand why they fight, we have been videotaping sibling fights so that we can better develop clinical strategies to reduce sibling conflict. Based on previous research, we have developed a theoretical framework covering the factors that are likely to contribute to sibling conflict which we are testing. These factors include: temperamental characteristics of the siblings themselves, characteristics of the parent-sibling relationship, characteristics of the broader family system, and the interactions among these factors. We propose a multifaceted approach to reducing sibling conflict that takes into account all of these factors and their interactions.

What makes brothers and sisters fuss and fight? Parents have probably been asking that question for as long as there have been families, and there is probably no simple answer. One of the main reasons we became interested in this area of conflict between siblings is that when you ask parents to list the things in

Gene H. Brody is Professor of Child and Family Development and Zolinda Stoneman is Professor of Child and Family Development at the University of Georgia, Athens, GA 30602. Dr. Brody and Dr. Stoneman participate in the Program for the Study of Competence in Children and Families.

This paper was supported by Grant BNS-84-15505 awarded by the National Science Foundation and Grant MH 40704 awarded by the National Institute of Mental Health.

39

their family that are troubling to them, the problem that almost always tops the list, especially for mothers, is "my kids fight all the time." Altogether, conflict and dissention among siblings has been repeatedly found to be one of the most common and persistent child-related problems facing families (Clifford, 1959; Kelly & Main, 1979; Leitenberg, Burchard, Burchard, Fuller & Lysaght, 1977).

Unfortunately, researchers and interventionists have tended to overlook the importance of the sibling relationship. Riskin and France (1972) noted the lack of research on sibling interaction in the family therapy literature. Family therapists have, at best, viewed sibling relationships as the products of interaction between each individual child and the parents rather than *among* the children themselves (Bank & Kahn, 1973). The neglect of the "sibling underworld," as Bank and Kahn (1973) have called it, is also notable in the clinical study of family behavior. Such studies have primarily used siblings as "normal" controls for maladjusted brothers and sisters or as a means of studying the "contagion" of psychopathology (Alanin, 1966; Hoover & Franz, 1972; Lidz, Fleck, Alanin & Cornelison, 1963; Lu, 1961; Meissner, 1970; Newman, 1966; Pollack, Woerner, Goldberg & Klein, 1969; Samuels & Chase, 1974; Stabenau, Tupin, Werner & Pollin, 1965; Wynne, Ryckoff, Day & Hirsch, 1958; Wynne & Singer, 1963). The aforementioned studies, however, provide little information on the causes of conflict in the sibling relationship.

Using in-home observations, we have been watching siblings fight to understand why they fight, so we can discover the kinds of clinical strategies that might reduce sibling conflict. Based on previous research, we have developed a theoretical framework covering the factors that are likely to contribute to sibling conflict which we are testing. These factors include:

1. Temperamental characteristics of the siblings: specifically, high activity level and impulsivity;
2. Characteristics of the parent-sibling relationship: differential treatment of siblings, intervention in sibling conflicts, and lack of clarity concerning rules and expectations of desired sibling behavior;

3. Characteristics of the broader family system: personal maladjustment in either parent, marital conflict, and an unhealthy emotional climate in the family; and
4. Interactions among any of the above factors. For example, unequal treatment of one sibling may be more damaging if that sibling is more temperamentally active and impulsive.

In this paper, we will review the evidence in support of our theoretical framework, report a study testing some of the factors proposed as contributory to sibling conflict, and finally suggest some recommendations, for reducing sibling conflict.

TEMPERAMENTAL CHARACTERISTICS OF THE SIBLINGS THEMSELVES

Previous research suggested that the temperamental characteristics of each sibling could play an important role in fostering sibling conflict. In its usual definition, this term refers to that portion of personality that is controlled by genetic or congenital factors. In practice, one cannot identify the specific portion of a temperamental characteristic (e.g., a child's activity level, emotional reactivity, or sociability) that is innate.

Because several of the major temperamental dimensions cannot be reliably assessed at birth, these dimensions can be assumed to be, in part, a product of the child's experiences, including the history of family interaction. With this in mind, we propose that sibling dyads are at risk for conflicted relationships when at least one child is highly active or impulsive. Additive effects are also anticipated; more conflict should take place in dyads in which both children are active and impulsive than in those containing only one such child.

Support for the hypothesis that the child's temperament affects sibling relationships can be found in studies of children who display *externalizing* types of behavioral problems (undercontrolled). These studies have compared the socially aggressive and negative behaviors exhibited by "non-problem" siblings with those of the identified problem child. In general, high correlations between siblings' rates of negative behavior have been reported (Arnold, Levine & Patterson, 1975; Mash & Johnston, 1983; Patterson, 1977). Extreme examples of punitive, destructive sibling relations can be found in the clinic families described by Patterson (1980). These problem children were involved in frequent aggressive exchanges with siblings. When one sibling initiated an antagonistic exchange, the other responded in kind with a highly negative behavior. Mash and Johnston (1983) found sibling conflict to be a major problem for high active-impulsive children. The sibling interactions of these children were characterized by approximately four times the amount of negative behavior as controls and approximately twice as much negative behavior as controls when being supervised by their mothers. These high rates of negative behavior in sibling dyads with a high active-impulsive child were unrelated to the sex or ordinal position of the high active child's sibling. The findings of these studies support our expectation: sibling dyads which include a high active-impulsive child tend to experience more conflict.

A highly active and impulsive brother or sister may affect the sibling relationship in different ways, depending on the ways in which parents manage their children. Some parents may relate to the children in ways that tend to increase sibling conflict, whereas others may use tactics that will decrease fighting. We believe, therefore, that no single factor determines the quality of the sibling relationship. Rather, we propose that the extent to which the children's own characteristics "fit" well into the larger family system affects their family relationships. This approach emphasizes the matches or mismatches that are created by the meshing of particular child characteristics with particular parent and family characteristics. Sameroff and Chandler (1975), Thomas and Chess (1981), and Lerner and Spanier (1978) have suggested similar approaches.

CHARACTERISTICS OF THE PARENT-SIBLING RELATIONSHIP

According to our theoretical framework, sibling pairs of similar temperament will respond differently to conflict depending on whether their parents adopt strategies that foster positive sibling relationships. Following is our concept of effective parenting strategies for managing sibling relations. We propose that the use of these strategies by parents will result in less conflicted sibling relationships even for at-risk sibling dyads. These effective strategies include: (a) equal treatment of siblings, (b) nonintervention in sibling conflict, and (c) clear rules and expectations for sibling behavior.

Equal Treatment of Siblings

Several theories suggest that differential treatment of siblings by parents may have negative effects. Social learning theory (Bandura, 1977) and equity theory (Adams, 1965; Walster, Berscheid & Walster, 1973) stress the relative amounts of social rewards that each child perceives he or she is receiving from the parents compared to the amount received by a sibling. Psychoanalytic theory (Freud, 1949) focuses on rivalry within the family among siblings competing for parental attention. Self-esteem maintenance theory (Tesser, 1980) hypothesizes that siblings' perceptions of differential treatment by their parents creates conflicted relations.

In view of its theoretical importance, it is surprising that the impact of differential treatment by parents has not been extensively investigated. A series of studies by Daniels and her colleagues has shown that adolescents and young adults believed they had experienced different treatment than their siblings in a wide variety of areas (Daniels & Plomin, 1985). In addition, they have found that parents perceive differences in their treatment of siblings in a wide variety of areas. In an observational study of school-aged sisters, Bryant & Crockenberg (1980) found that when one sister's needs were met by the mother while the other sister did not have her needs met, the sister whose needs were not met was less kind to her sibling.

Nonintervention in Sibling Conflict

Two very different theoretical orientations suggest that parental intervention increases sibling conflict. Dreikurs (1964) argues that children fight to gain their parents' attention. In order to do this, children will produce conflict situations hoping their parents will intervene, thus giving them the attention they desire.

Dreikurs (1964) further believes their parents do their children a disservice by intervening in sibling arguments. They provide inappropriate attention, thus increasing the likelihood of more fighting, as well as depriving their children of the opportunity to learn to resolve their own conflicts. Levi, Buskila, and Gerzi (1977) and Kelly and Main (1979) taught parents to stay out of fights between their children, and found that such nonintervention was a useful means of reducing sibling conflict. These two studies begin to establish an empirical foundation for Dreikurs' (1964) approach to sibling conflict. More research, however, is needed on these strategies.

Strategies drawn from a behavioral orientation have received more research attention. Allison and Allison (1971); Leitenberg et al. (1977); O'Leary, O'Leary, and Becker (1967) demonstrated that rewarding children for playing cooperatively, and sending them to time-out for fighting, effectively reduced sibling conflict.

Note that the behavioral approach recommends stopping the sibling fight using time-out techniques to separate the combatants, whereas Dreikurs (1964) (and Schachter & Stone, this volume) would favor letting the siblings settle their own arguments without stopping the fight. Dreikurs (1964) (and Schachter & Stone) would claim that allowing the siblings to settle their own conflicts can have long-term benefits for the sibling relationship, because it provides the opportunity to learn important conflict-resolution skills such as compromising and trading. At this time, no data are available to compare the long-term effects of these two different approaches. In the short-term both approaches seem to reduce sibling conflict.

Until long-term follow-up data is available, practitioners would do well to note that whether adopting Dreikurs' (1964) strategy of letting the siblings settle their own arguments or the behavioral strategy of stopping the fight, the parent does not become embroiled in the sibling conflict itself. The parent does not judge which sibling has the more valid claim, the parent does not take sides, and the parent does not suggest ways of resolving the conflict. Research indicates that this basic strategy of nonintervention reduces sibling conflict.

Clear Rules and Expectations for Sibling Behavior

Finally, a family's inability to set clear rules and expectations for sibling behavior contributes to conflicted relationships. The importance of providing children with clear statements of expectations has been demonstrated both in the laboratory (Roberts, McMahon, Forehand & Humphreys, 1978) and in treatment outcome studies (Peed, Roberts & Forehand, 1977). Most rules that parents provide in an effort to govern siblings' behavior toward one another consist of vague statements that do not specify the desired actions to be performed, thus creating an unclear situation for the sibling dyad. Classic vague rules include, "Play nicely together," "Be good children," "Be nice to your sister," etc. Although the parent probably has some specific behaviors in mind when issuing these rules, they are not described for the siblings. The consequence, at least from the parents' perspective, is usually conflict.

CHARACTERISTICS OF THE BROADER FAMILY SYSTEM

The parents' psychological adjustment and the family emotional climate will influence the way the parents manage the sibling relationship. In turn, sibling relations are expected to be less supportive and more conflicted when family support resources diminish to the point of damaging the integrity of the parent-sibling relationship. The clinical literature suggests that parental personal maladjustment, marital conflict, and an unhealthy family emotional climate are related to child psychopathology and behavioral difficulties.

Parental Personal Maladjustment

A number of investigators have reported that people with emotional disturbances do not function well as parents. Depressed mothers, for example, have been found to be less involved with and affectionate toward their children, feel more guilt and resentment, and generally experience more difficulty in managing and communicating with them than do nondepressed mothers (Anthony & Ittelson, 1980; Cohler, Grunebaum, Weiss, Hartman &

Gallant, 1976; Hops et al., 1985; Schulterbrandt & Raskin, 1977). In addition, these parents perceive themselves as ineffective (Forehand, Wells, McMahon, Griest & Rogers, 1982); and perceive their children as poorly adjusted (Brody & Forehand, 1986; Griest, Wells & Forehand, 1979).

Children whose parents are experiencing psychiatric problems frequently have emotional and behavioral problems themselves. Attention spans and relations with others are disrupted in both the infants and the school-aged children of psychiatrically disturbed parents (Gamer, Gallant, Grunebaum & Cohler, 1977; Neale & Weintraub, 1975; Sameroff, Barocas & Seifer, 1984). These children have been found to be poorly adjusted in school (Weintraub, Neale & Liebert, 1975), with their siblings (Beisser, Glasser & Grant, 1967) and with their peers (Conners, Himmelhoch, Goyette, Ulrich & Neil, 1979; Welner, Welner, McCrasy & Leonard, 1977). The behaviors they display are variously described in the literature as destructive, defiant, withdrawn, uncooperative, impatient, belligerent, and socially isolated. Although most of this research has focused on the children of severely disturbed parents, evidence is also available to indicate that the psychological adjustment of parents without psychiatric diagnoses or who are not in psychological treatment is related both to the children's adjustment and to the parent's perception of child adjustment.

Marital Conflict

Inspired by the family systems and therapy movement, clinical researchers from various persuasions have sought to establish a link between marital conflict and child psychological adjustment. After an extensive review of the literature, O'Leary and Emery (in press) concluded that marital conflict and child problems are generally related, and they are even more strongly related when the parent or child has psychological problems or the child is referred for psychological treatment. A review of eleven investigations involving nonclinic families (Block, Block & Morrison, 1981; Emery & O'Leary, 1984; Ferguson & Allen, 1978; Whitehead, 1979) led to the conclusion that marital problems are related to behavior problems especially those involving undercontrol, in both boys and girls. In clinic-referred samples, a strong relationship has been found between marital problems and under-controlled behavior in children, particularly boys (Oltmanns, Broderick & O'Leary, 1977). Other comparisons of families that include a disturbed school-aged child or adolescent with matched control families have found the former families to be character-ized by, among other problems, higher levels of interspousal conflict (Bell & Bell, 1982; Doane, 1978; Ferreira, 1963; Fis-cher, 1980; Jacob, 1975; Lewis, Rodnick, Michael & Goldstein, 1981; Minuchin, Rosman & Baker, 1978; Mishler & Waxler, 1968; Riskin & France, 1972; Shepperson, 1982; Westly & Ep-stein, 1969; Wynne, Jones & Al-Khayyal, 1982). Thus, evi-dence does exist to support a relationship between parents' mari-tal conflict and child functioning.

In the section that follows, we will summarize a large study designed to test some of the above factors, to see if they do in-deed contribute to sibling conflict. (A more detailed account of the methodology and a portion of the results is presented in a recent paper by the authors [Brody, Stoneman & Burke, 1986].) To test these factors, we obtained maternal ratings of child tem-perament, observed mother-sibling interactions for the unequal treatment of siblings by mothers, and obtained maternal and pa-ternal self-reports of marital adjustment and family emotional cli-mate. Each of these factors was correlated with the sibling con-flict that we observed in the children's own homes.

STUDYING SIBLING CONFLICT

Method

Subjects

Forty mothers and fathers and their same-sex children, 20 pairs of boys and 20 pairs of girls, participated in the study. The older siblings were 7 to 9 years old and the younger children were 4 to 6 years old. All the children were from two-child, Caucasian, middle- and upper-middle-class families in which both biological parents were present in the home.

Procedure

Mothers and siblings were videotaped in their living rooms on two separate occasions. On one visit mothers were videotaped interacting with both children, and on the other visit only the siblings were videotaped. Mother-sibling threesomes and sibling twosomes were observed while playing with a popular board game and a set of construction materials. Family members were asked to play with the toys just as they would if the videotape camera was not present. Three sibling behaviors were assessed: total verbal interactions, positive/supportive behavior, and negative/aggressive behavior. Four maternal behaviors were assessed: total verbalizations, positive/negative, and managing behavior.

In addition to these observational measures, a questionnaire was administered to each mother to evaluate each child's temperament. This instrument, a modified version of one designed by Thomas and Chess (1977), measures temperament dimensions in children 3 through 9 years of age. Activity (motoric vigor), emotional intensity (amount of emotional energy or vigor expressed in a variety of situations), and persistence (attention span and continuation of tasks despite obstacles) were evaluated. Marital functioning was also assessed by questionnaires that each parent completed. Marital consensus, affection, cohesion, and satisfaction were evaluated.

In addition, both parents completed a questionnaire based on one developed by Moos (1974) that assessed the social climate in the family. Cohesion (the degree of commitment, help, and support that family members feel from each other), expressiveness (the extent to which family members act openly and express feelings directly), and conflict (the amount of openly expressed anger, aggression, and conflict among family members) were measured.

Results

Does the child's temperament, the unequal treatment of siblings by the mother, and/or the emotional climate of the family correlate with the amount of conflicted behavior shown by each sibling?

Child temperament and sibling conflict. In female sibling

pairs, highly active older sisters behaved more antagonistically toward their younger sisters. Similarly, highly active younger sisters behaved more antagonistically toward their older sisters, who in turn behaved antagonistically toward them. Both younger and older sisters who were rated as more emotionally intense also behaved more antagonistically toward their siblings, who reciprocated the negative treatment. By contrast, a high persistence rating for either sibling (indicating low impulsivity) was associated with lower levels of antagonistic behavior for both siblings. In male sibling pairs, high activity in a younger brother was associated with more antagonistic behavior from both siblings. Older male siblings with high emotional intensity ratings received more antagonistic behavior from their younger brothers. By contrast, when the younger brother received a high persistence rating, both brothers directed less antagonistic behavior toward one another.

Maternal differential treatment of siblings and sibling conflict. Maternal differential treatment of the siblings was an impressive predictor of the quality of sibling relations. When mothers talked more to the younger child, the siblings were less likely to talk to each other or to be positive and supportive with each other. The more mothers favored the younger child with positive behavior, the less positively the siblings behaved toward each other. When mothers directed more management behaviors toward their younger children, the younger siblings spoke less and behaved less negatively toward the older sibling. When the temperament ratings for each child were controlled, the results did not change, indicating that child temperament was not responsible for the association between unequal treatment of siblings and sibling interactions. Both the temperament of each sibling and maternal unequal treatment appear to affect sibling interactions independently.

Family emotional climate and sibling conflict. Levels of sibling conflict observed while the children were playing alone were related to the family emotional climate. Older siblings whose parents reported less enjoyment with one another, lower levels of marital satisfaction, and more family conflict displayed more antagonistic behavior. A similar pattern was found among younger siblings. Higher levels of negative behavior were associated with less parental agreement over family decisions, less affection between parents, lower parental marital satisfaction, and higher ratings of family conflict. Thus, these data suggest that other family relationships, particularly the parents' marital relationship, affect the quality of sibling relationships.

CONCLUSIONS

In this paper, we have proposed a theoretical framework covering the factors that might contribute to sibling conflict which includes temperamental characteristics of the siblings, characteristics of the parent-sibling relationship, characteristics of the broader family system, and the interaction between these factors. A number of these factors have been tested and have been validated. Research is continuing. In the meantime, we recommend a multifaceted approach to reducing sibling conflict that takes into consideration all the units and sub-systems within the family, the family system as a whole, and their interactions. Specifically, the following recommendations seem warranted:

1. Regarding child temperament, clinicians and educators should be alerted to expect more sibling conflict among children who are temperamentally more active and impulsive.
2. Regarding parent-sibling relationships, strategies that foster equal treatment of siblings, discourage parents from intervening in their children's conflicts, and encourage parents to set clear rules and expectations for sibling behavior, all promise to decrease sibling conflict.
3. Regarding the emotional climate of the family, the data suggest that efforts aimed at resolving marital conflict can greatly enhance the quality of the sibling relationship; the less marital conflict, the less sibling conflict.

REFERENCES

Adams, J. S. (1965). Inequity in social exchange. In L. Berkowitz (Ed.), *Advances in experimental social psychology*, Vol. 2. New York: Academic Press.

Alanin, Y. O. (1966). The mothers of schizophrenic patients. *Scandinavian Acta Psychiatry and Neurology, 33*. (Supplement 2) (pp. 1-89).

Allison, T. S. & Allison, S. L. (1971). Time out from reinforcement: Effect on sibling aggression. *The Psychological Record, 21,* 81-86.

Anthony, E. J. & Ittleson, B. F. (1980). The effects of maternal depression on the infant. Paper presented at the Symposium on Infant Psychiatry III, San Francisco.

Arnold, J., Levine, A. & Patterson, G. R. (1975). Changes in sibling behavior following intervention. *Journal of Consulting and Clinical Psychology, 43,* 683-688.

Bandura, A. (1977). *Social learning theory.* Englewood Cliffs, NJ: Prentice-Hall.

Bank, S. P. & Kahn, M. D. (1973). *The sibling bond.* New York: Basic Books.

Beisser, A., Glasser, N. & Grant, M. (1967). Psychosocial adjustment in children of schizophrenic mothers. *Journal of Nervous and Mental Disease, 145,* 429-440.

Bell, L. G. & Bell, D. C. (1982). Family climate and the role of the female adolescent: Determinants of adolescent functioning. *Family Relations, 31,* 519-527.

Block, J. H., Block, J. & Morrison, A. (1981). Parental agreement-disagreement on child-rearing orientations and gender-related personality correlates in children. *Child Development, 52,* 965-974.

Brody, G. H. & Forehand, R. (1986). Maternal perceptions of child maladjustment as a function of the combined influence of child behavior and maternal depression. *Journal of Consulting and Clinical Psychology, 54,* 237-240.

Brody, G. H., Stoneman, Z. & Burke, M. (1986). Child temperaments, maternal differential behavior, and sibling relations. Unpublished manuscript. Dawson Hall, University of Georgia, Athens, GA 30602.

Bryant, B. & Crockenberg, S. (1980). Correlates and dimensions of prosocial behavior: A study of female siblings with their mothers. *Child Development, 43,* 282-287.

Clifford, E. (1959). Discipline in the home: A controlled observational study of parental practices. *Journal of Genetic Psychology, 95,* 45-82.

Conners, C. K., Himmelhoch, J., Goyette, C. H., Ulrich, R. & Neil, J. F. (1979). Children of parents with affective illness. *Journal of the American Academy of Child Psychiatry, 18,* 600-607.

Daniels, D. & Plomin, R. (1985). Differential experience of siblings in the same family. *Developmental Psychology, 21,* 747-760.

Doane, J. A. (1978). Family interaction and communication deviance in disturbed and normal families: A review of research. *Family Process, 17,* 357-376.

Dreikurs, R. (1964). *Children the challenge.* New York: Hawthorne Books.

Emery, R. E. & O'Leary, K. S. (1984). Marital discord and child behavior problems in a nonclinic sample. *Journal of Abnormal Child Psychology, 12,* 411-420.

Ferguson, L. R. & Allen, D. R. (1978). Congruence of parent perception, marital satisfaction, and child adjustment. *Journal of Consulting and Clinical Psychology, 46,* 345-346.

Ferreira, A. (1963). Decision making in normal and pathologic families. *Archives of General Psychiatry, 8,* 68-73.

Fischer, J. L. (1980). Reciprocity, agreement, and family style in family systems with a disturbed and nondisturbed adolescent. *Journal of Youth and Adolescence, 10,* 391-406.

Forehand, R., Wells, K. C., McMahon, R. J., Griest, D. & Rogers, T. (1982). Maternal perceptions of maladjustment in clinic-referred children: An extension of earlier research. *Journal of Behavioral Assessment, 4,* 145-151.

Freud, S. (1949). *An outline of psychoanalysis.* New York: Norton. (Originally published 1940).

Garner, E., Gallant, D., Grunebaum, H. & Cohler, B. J. (1977). Children of psychotic mothers. *Archives of General Psychiatry, 34,* 592-597.

Griest, D., Wells, K. C. & Forchand, R. (1979). An examination of predictors of maternal perceptions of maladjustment in clinic-referred children. *Journal of Abnormal Psychology, 89*, 497-500.

Hoover, C. F. & Franz, J. D. (1972). Siblings in the families of schizophrenics. *Archives of General Psychiatry, 26*, 334-342.

Hops, J., Brglan, A., Sherman, L., Arthur, J., Friedman, L. & Osteen, V. (1985). Home observations of family interactions of depressed women. Unpublished manuscript, Oregon Research Institute.

Jacob, T. (1975). Family interaction in disturbed and normal families: A methodological and substantive review. *Psychological Bulletin, 82*, 33-65.

Kelly, F. D. & Main, F. O. (1979). Sibling conflict in a single-parent family: An empirical case study. *American Journal of Family Therapy, 7*, 39-47.

Leitenberg, H., Burchard, J. D., Burchard, S. M., Fuller, E. J. & Lysaght, T.V. (1977). Using positive reinforcement to suppress behavior: Some experimental comparisons with sibling conflict. *Behavior Therapy, 8*, 168-182.

Lerner, R. M. & Spanier, G. B. (1978). *Child influences on marital and family interaction: A lifespan perspective*. New York: Academic Press.

Levi, A. M., Buskila, M. & Gerzi, S. (1977). Benign neglect: Reducing fights among siblings. *Journal of Individual Psychology, 33*, 240-245.

Lewis, J. M., Rodnick, E. H., Michael, J. & Goldstein, M. (1981). Intra-familial interaction behavior, parental communication deviance, and risk for schizophrenia. *Journal of Abnormal Psychology, 90*, 448-457.

Lidz, T., Fleck, S., Alanin, Y. O. & Cornelison, A. R. (1963). Schizophrenic patients and their siblings. *Psychiatry, 26*, 1-18.

Lu, Y. (1961). Mother-child role relations in schizophrenia: A comparison of schizophrenic patients with nonschizophrenic siblings. *Psychiatry, 24*, 133-142.

Mash, E. J. & Johnston, C. (1983). Sibling interactions of hyperactive and normal children and their relationship to reports of maternal stress and self-esteem. *Journal of Clinical Child Psychology, 12*, 91-99.

Meissner, W. W. (1970). Sibling relations in the schizophrenic family. *Family Process, 9*, 1-25.

Minuchin, S., Rosman, B. L. & Baker, L. (1978). *Psychosomatic families*. Cambridge, MA: Harvard University Press.

Mishler, E. & Waxler, N. (1968). *Interaction in families: An experimental study of family processes and schizophrenia*. New York: Wiley.

Moos, R. H. (1974). *Preliminary manual for the Family Environment Scale*. Palo Alto: Consulting Psychologists Press, Inc.

Neale, J. M. & Weintraub, S. (1975). Children vulnerable to psychopathology: The Stony Brook High-Risk Project. *Journal of Abnormal Child Psychology, 3*, 95-113.

Newman, G. (1966). Younger brothers of schizophrenics. *Psychiatry, 29*, 146-151.

O'Leary, K. D. & Emery, R. E. (1984). Marital discord and child behavior problems. In M. D. Levine & P. Satz (Eds.), *Developmental variations and dysfunction* (pp. 91-122). New York: Academic Press.

O'Leary, K., O'Leary, D. & Becker, B. (1967). Modification of a deviant sibling interaction pattern in the home. *Behavior Research and Therapy, 5*, 113-126.

Oltmanns, T. F., Broderick, J. E. & O'Leary, K. D. (1977). Marital adjustment and the efficacy of behavior therapy with children. *Journal of Consulting and Clinical Psychology, 45*, 724-729.

Patterson, G. R. (1977). Accelerating stimuli for two classes of coercive behaviors. *Journal of Abnormal Child Psychology, 5*, 335-350.

Patterson, G. R. (1980). The unacknowledged victims. *Monographs for the Society for Research in Child Development, 45* (5, Whole No. 186).

Peed, S., Roberts, M. & Forehand, R. (1977). Evaluation of the effectiveness of standardized parent training program in altering the interaction of mothers and their noncompliant children. *Behavior Modification, 1*, 323-350.

Pollack, M., Woerner, M. G., Goldberg, M. & Klein, D. F. (1969). Siblings of schizophrenic and nonschizophrenic psychiatric patients. *Archives of General Psychiatry, 20*, 650-658.

Riskin, J. & France, E. (1972). An evaluative review of family interaction research. *Family Process, 11*, 365-456.

Roberts, M. W., McMahon, R. J., Forehand, R. & Humphreys, L. (1978). The effects of parental instruction-giving on child compliance. *Behavior Therapy, 9*, 793-798.

Sameroff, A. J., Barocas, R. & Seifer, R. (1984). The early development of children born to mentally ill women. In N. F. Watt, E. J. Anthony, L. C. Wynne & J. Rolf (Eds.), *Children at risk for schizophrenia* (pp. 27-54). New York: Cambridge University Press.

Sameroff, A. J. & Chandler, M. J. (1975). Reproductive risk and the continuum of caretaking casualty. In F. D. Horowitz (Ed.), *Review of child development research* (Vol. 4). Chicago: University of Chicago Press.

Samuels, L. & Chase, L. (1974). The well siblings of schizophrenics. *American Journal of Family Therapy, 7*, 24-35.

Schulterbrandt, J. G. & Raskin, A. (1977). *Depression in children – diagnosis, treatment and concept models.* New York: Raven Press.

Shepperson, V. L. (1982). Differences in assertion and aggression between normal and neurotic family triads. *Journal of Personality Assessment, 46*, 409-414.

Stabenau, J., Tupin, J., Werner, M. & Pollin, W. (1965). A comparative study of families of schizophrenics, delinquents, and normals. *Psychiatry, 28*, 45-59.

Tesser, A. (1980). Self-esteem maintenance in family dynamics. *Journal of Personality and Social Psychology, 39*, 77-91.

Thomas, A. & Chess, S. (1981). *Dynamics of psychological development.* New York: Brunner/Mazel.

Walster, E., Berscheid, E. & Walster, G. W. (1973). New directions in equity research. *Journal of Personality and Social Psychology, 25*, 151-176.

Weintraub, S., Neale, J. M. & Liebert, D. E. (1975). Teacher ratings of children vulnerable to psychopathology. *American Journal of Orthopsychiatry, 45*, 839-945.

Welner, Z., Welner, A., McCrary, M. D. & Leonard, M. A. (1977). Psychopathology in children of inpatients with depression – A controlled study. *Journal of Nervous and Mental Disease, 164*, 408-413.

Westley, W. A. & Epstein, N. B. (1969). *The silent majority.* San Francisco: Jossey-Bass.

Whitehead, L. (1979). Sex differences in children's responses to family stress: A re-evaluation. *Journal of Child Psychology and Psychiatry, 20*, 247-254.

Wynne, L. C., Jones, J. E. & Al-Khayyal, M. (1982). Healthy family communication patterns: Observations in families "at risk" for psychopathology. In F. Walsh (Ed.), *Normal family processes* (142-167). New York: Guilford.

Wynne, L., Ryckoff, I., Day, J. & Hirsch, S. (1958). Pseudo-mutuality in the family relations of schizophrenics. *Psychiatry, 21*, 205-220.

Wynne, L. C. & Singer, M. T. (1963). Thought disorder and family relations of schizophrenics: A research strategy. *Archives of General Psychiatry, 9*, 191-198.

Comparing and Contrasting Siblings: Defining the Self

Frances Fuchs Schachter, PhD
Richard K. Stone, MD

SUMMARY. Siblings tend to be defined as different or contrasting, a phenomenon called *sibling deidentification*. Normal sibling deidentification seems to be the product of conflict resolution and reconciliation with each sibling developing different identities in order to mitigate the constant competition and comparison that comes with sibling rivalry. On the other hand, in pathological deidentification, the natural flow of sibling conflict and reconciliation seems obstructed as one sibling is assigned the fixed identity of "devil" constantly harassing the other sibling defined as "angel" and parents are constantly intervening to protect the angel-victim. A clinical strategy designed to restore the flow of conflict and reconciliation is proposed in the treatment and prevention of psychopathology.

One of the most startling findings in the new field of behavioral genetics is that siblings tend to be almost as different from each other in personality as are children from different families despite their shared genes and their shared home, school, and community environments (Rowe & Plomin, 1981; Scarr & Grajek, 1982). This finding is all the more surprising because developmental research on siblings has focused on sibling similarity, that is, on sibling imitation, modeling, or identification. Until recently, sibling differences have been virtually ignored. Rowe

Frances Fuchs Schachter is Associate Professor of Pediatrics, New York Medical College and Supervising Pediatric Psychologist, Metropolitan Hospital Center, 1901 First Avenue, Room 523, New York, NY 10029. Richard K. Stone is Professor of Clinical Pediatrics, New York Medical College and Chief of the Pediatric Service, Metropolitan Hospital Center, and may be reached at the same address.

and Elam will have more to stay about the origins of these sibling differences in their paper (this volume) on heredity and environment. This paper will focus on one phenomenon that is bound to contribute to an understanding of why siblings are so different from each other, namely, they tend to define themselves as different or contrasting and so do their parents (e.g., one sibling the extrovert, the other the introvert; one active, the other passive; one the angel, the other the devil; one the easy child, the other the difficult child). We call this phenomenon of sibling contrast *sibling deidentification* (Schachter, Gilutz, Shore & Adler, 1978; Schachter, Shore, Feldman-Rotman, Marquis & Campbell, 1976).

Whether one is defined as an extrovert, an introvert, as active or passive, ordinarily does not have implications for one's mental health. On the other hand, whether one is defined as an angel or devil, or as an easy or difficult child often does. It is the extremes of bad and good that we normally associate with psychopathology (Offord & Waters, 1983), externalizing psychopathology including delinquency and conduct disorders with the former and internalizing psychopathology including perfectionism, shyness, inhibition and somatic complaints with the latter (Achenbach, 1982). Thus, there seem to be normal and pathological forms of sibling deidentification with important implications for those who work with troubled children. We will report the highlights of our basic research on normal samples (Schachter et al., 1976, 1978) and then describe how the concept of sibling deidentification might be applied in clinical settings in the treatment and prevention of psychopathology (Schachter, 1985; Schachter & Stone, 1985).

BASIC FINDINGS: "DIFFERENT AS DAY AND NIGHT"

Research on sibling deidentification was inspired by such commonplace statements as "My sister is entirely different from me" or "My two children are as different as day and night." Such statements seemed to be as common in everyday conversation as "He (or she) is just like his (or her) mother (or father)." Yet, although research on child-parent identification was voluminous, research on sibling deidentification was virtually nonexistent.

We began by simply asking university students in two-child families if they were alike or different from their siblings in overall personality. In this way, we sought to confirm the everyday observation that siblings tend to define themselves as different from each other. Moreover, we set out to see if defining oneself as different from one's sibling was correlated with any of the traditional sibling-status variables, birth order, spacing, or sex of sibling. If we could establish a link between the incidence of sibling deidentification and any of these variables, we might begin to understand why deidentification takes place. In the case of pathological deidentification, understanding might suggest clinical strategies to induce change.

In pilot studies, we drew three successive samples of students in two-child families. In all three samples, subjects reported that they were different from their siblings about twice as often as they reported being alike, but there was no consistent correlation between sibling deidentification and any of the traditional sibling-status variables. Firstborn siblings were just as likely to define themselves as different from second-borns as vice versa. Nor did spacing or sex of sibling show consistent effects.

The results of these preliminary studies were both encouraging and discouraging. On the one hand, they provided statistical proof that sibling deidentification was indeed a common human experience, far more common than defining oneself as being like one's sibling. On the other hand, the data provided no clues as to why deidentification occurs. Unless we could identify conditions associated with increases or decreases in the incidence of sibling deidentification, we could shed no light on why it occurs.

Not until we departed from the customary procedure of studying sibling pairs in two-child families and began studying pairs in three-child families as well, did the findings fall into a consistent pattern suggesting a promising hypothesis. Two- and three-child families yield four types of sibling pairs, the first- and second-born in the two-child family (SIB 1-2), the first- and second-born in three child family (also SIB 1-2), and the second- and third-born (SIB 2-3) and first- and third-born (SIB 1-3) in the three-child family. With four types of sibling pairs, it becomes possible not only to study the effects of birth order, spacing, and sex of sibling on the incidence of sibling deidentification *within* each class of sibling pair, but also to examine variations in the incidence of deidentification *between* different classes of sibling pairs. For example, we can assess whether deidentification is more common in SIB 1-2 pairs than in SIB 2-3 or SIB 1-3 pairs.

To compare the incidence of deidentification among these four classes of sibling pairs, we collected large samples of two- and three-child families. First, we studied 383 undergraduates asking if they were alike or different from their siblings in overall personality (Schachter et al., 1976). Then we studied 140 mothers asking for each pair of their children (average age = 6 years) if they were alike or different from each other (Schachter et al., 1978).

The results were consistent as can be seen in Table 1. For both samples, sibling deidentification was found to be widespread in SIB 1-2 pairs whether in two- or three-child families and considerably less common in SIB 2-3 and SIB 1-3 pairs. Moreover, there were no significant differences between SIB 2-3 and SIB 1-3 pairs. The data indicate that sibling deidentification occurs mainly in the first two children in the family including families with only two children.[1]

Why does deidentification occur mainly in the first pair of children in the family? Before attempting to answer this question, we will report on the effect of birth order, spacing, and sex of sibling within each class of sibling pair. For this set of traditional sibling-status variables, the only statistically significant finding was a paradoxical one, that is, the reverse of what one might expect. For each sample, one of the four classes of pairs showed deidentification to be significantly more common in same-sex siblings than in opposite-sex, whereas none showed significantly more contrast for opposite-sex siblings. Significantly greater contrast for same-sex siblings is a paradox because the weight of genetic and cultural factors, including sexual stereotypes, might lead one to expect significantly more contrast for opposite-sex siblings. Yet, it is the same-sex siblings who are more often defined as different.[2] Why does deidentification favor same-sex siblings and why does it occur mainly in the first pair of

TABLE 1

Percentage of Sibling Deidentification in Sibling Pairs

of Undergraduate and Mother Samples

Sibling Pairs	Percentage	n
Undergraduate Sample		
Two-child-family (SIB 1-2)	62.2	180
Three-child-family		
SIB 1-2	75.3	154
SIB 2-3	52.7	112
SIB 1-3	45.3	139
Mother Sample		
Two-child-family (SIB 1-2)	80.0	95
Three-child-family		
SIB 1-2	90.9	44
SIB 2-3	65.9	44
SIB 1-3	57.8	45

Note. The data in column 1 are from "Sibling Deidentification" by F.F. Schachter, E. Shore, S. Feldman-Rotman, R.E. Marquis, & S. Campbell, 1976, *Developmental Psychology*, 12, p. 421. Copyright 1976 by the American Psychological Association. The data in column 2 are from "Sibling Deidentification Judged by Mothers: Cross-validation and Developmental Studies" by F.F. Schachter, G. Gilutz, E. Shore, & M. Adler, 1978, *Child Development*, 49, p. 544. Copyright 1978 by the Society for Research in Child Development. Reprinted by permission.

children in the family? It is these two findings that any theory of sibling deidentification must explain.

Rivalry-Defense Hypothesis: Mitigating Competition and Avoiding Comparison

The pattern of occurrence of sibling deidentification suggests that it is designed to mitigate sibling rivalry as incidence is highest where sibling rivalry is expected to be most intense. The first two children in the family are likely to be the most rivalrous since competition, comparison and conflict are undiluted by the inevitable delay in the arrival of the third-born. Similarly, same-sex siblings are more likely to compete or be compared than are opposite-sex siblings because of a common core of shared desires and attributes. Deidentification could help make these conflicts manageable. By expressing themselves in different ways and in different spheres, siblings are spared the necessity of constantly defending their turf against incursions from each other. Negative feelings abate, strengthening the bonds of love between them.

We call this rivalry-defense process the *Cain Complex* by analogy with the Oedipus Complex. In the latter case, child-parent rivalry is assumed to be resolved by the child identifying with the parent. In the case of the Cain Complex, sibling rivalry appears to be resolved by the siblings deidentifying with each other.

Bossard and Boll (1956) have proposed an alternative theory to explain why siblings adopt different personality roles, as they describe it. Based on observations of large families, they suggest that children in these families must struggle to establish a distinctive identity to avoid being lost in the crowd of other siblings. The present findings indicate that the risk of being lost in the crowd is not enough to explain why siblings define themselves as different. First, sibling deidentification is more common in sibling pairs of small two-child families than it is in some sibling pairs (SIB 2-3 and SIB 1-3) of larger three-child families although the risk of being lost in a crowd of siblings is greater for the latter. Additionally, deidentification is more common in the first pair of siblings in three-child families than in other pairs although the size of the "crowd" of siblings is the same for all three siblings.

By contrast, the rivalry-defense hypothesis can account for these findings. Moreover, the hypothesis is supported by experimental research on social comparison theory.

Social comparison theory (Festinger, 1954; Suls & Miller, 1977) postulates that for the purposes of survival we need to develop a realistic picture of ourselves and that when there are no objective criteria to do so (e.g., "I can throw a ball 10 feet."), we learn about ourselves by a process of comparing ourselves to others. To take a familiar example, when a student obtains a raw score of 121 on a test, this tells him or her nothing about him or herself until he knows how his/her score compares with those of others taking the test. Yet, although it may be necessary to compare ourselves to others to learn about who we are, it can nevertheless be a painful experience. In the natural course of events, social comparison is likely to demonstrate that one party is superior and the other inferior, one better, the other worse. Since this information is likely to breed resentment, envy and a loss of self-esteem on the part of the inferior one, and guilt, fear of loss of love and the need to hide one's delight on the part of the superior one, both parties must be prepared to cope with a flood of negative feelings if they do not wish to jeopardize their ongoing relationship.

Laboratory studies of social comparison have demonstrated that these disruptive feelings can be mitigated by making the other different from oneself so that he/she becomes noncomparable. In this way, painful comparison can be avoided. For example, Mettee and Riskind (1974) have demonstrated that subjects feel more favorably toward a superior-performing other when the latter is promoted to a higher ability level, a level so different that it places the other in a noncomparable category. Making the other dissimilar and noncomparable also makes him or her less threatening to the self. Similarly, Nadler, Jazwinski, and Lau (1976) found that males who were rejected by females in favor of another male felt better about themselves and disliked the other male less, if they thought the other male was dissimilar to themselves.

These studies (plus a number of related ones [see Brickman & Bulman, 1977]) provide experimental support for the hypothesis that defining oneself as different from one's sibling, can serve to diminish the costs of sibling rivalry, of constant competition and comparison. Deidentification can diminish the costs to the relationship itself in that siblings are apt to like each other better. It can also diminish the costs to the siblings in that their self-esteem is less likely to be threatened.

Developmental Course

It will come as no surprise to those working with preschoolers that almost all of them (84.4%), when observed in their school setting for 15 minutes each, produced some kind of social comparison statement, for example, "I can run faster than you;" "My spaceship is higher than yours" (Mosatche & Bragonier, 1981, p. 377). More to the point, Dunn and Kendrick (1982) note that 2, 3, and 4 year olds often compare themselves with their sibling in their everyday conversation, many doing so shortly after the birth of their sibling.

Apparently, children compare themselves with others from an early age, perhaps especially with their siblings who are constantly available for comparison. At what age then does this social-comparison information begin to be used as a basis for defining a stable self-concept? Research on the development of the self (Harter, 1983) and on the role of social comparison in this development (Aboud, 1985; Ruble, Boggiano, Feldman & Loebl, 1980) suggests that this process starts to stabilize at the beginning of the school years when children become capable of seeing the world from the perspective of the other, not just from their own perspective.

What about deidentification? When does it begin? The developmental data so far collected are limited. We have replicated the undergraduate findings on high school students (unpublished), but have not yet asked school-age or preschool children whether they are alike or different from their siblings. (Preschoolers may not grasp the question). On the other hand, our mother sample provides interesting developmental data (Schachter et al., 1978). As can be seen in Figure 1, based on mother judgments of their two children as "different" or "opposite," sibling deidentification shows a linear increment from near-chance levels in the first years of life to near-universal levels by age 6 when it stabilizes.

In summary, data on normal samples indicate that the tendency to define siblings as contrasting begins at an early age, that it is widespread in the first two children in a family (including families with only two children), and that, in the event of significant differences, it is more common in same-sex siblings than in opposite-sex. Additionally, although our research so far has cen-

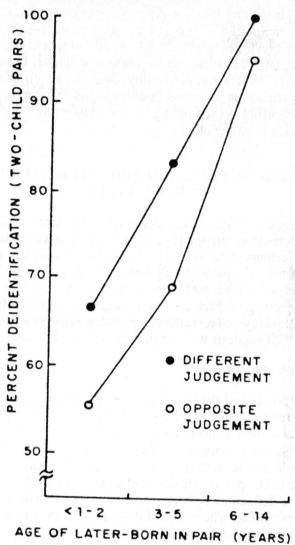

FIGURE 1. Percentage deidentification for mother's alike-different and same-opposite judgements of their two children with the younger child ranging in age from 3 weeks to 14 years. *Note*. From "Siblings Deidentification Judged by Mothers: Cross-Validation and Developmental Studies" by F. F. Schachter, G. Gilutz, E. Shore, M. Adler, 1978, *Child Development*, *49*, p. 545. Copyright 1978 by the Society for Research in Child Development, Inc. Reprinted by permission.

cuss the topic. Why does favoritism start? Why does it continue in some families, while in others it is blunted or neutralized, its sting removed by warmth and humor? Finally, what can we learn about ordinary favoritism from an intensive clinical analysis of its extreme manifestations?

Favoritism and its cohort, rejection, can first be understood through the special prism of psychoanalytic ideas. The concept of *projective identification* helps to explain why some parents have peculiar emotional reactions to apparently neutral or harmless physical or behavioral characteristics of children.[1] "One can have violent or fearful emotional reactions [or loving, tender reactions] toward those others who *most* remind one of upsetting aspects of oneself" (Bank & Kahn, 1982). When an infant begins kicking in the womb, for example, the parent may project such diverse qualities as: strength, independence, masculinity, or such disparaging attributes as aggressiveness, nastiness, or anxiety.[1] No two parents' projections about an infant's behavior are the same because no two parents' histories are the same. Understanding favoritism and its eventual route to sibling rivalry requires knowing how the parents interpret the child's existence through their own experiences. As psychoanalytic writers point out, the ways in which parents attribute motives of good and bad to children are not consciously thought out. The parents are likely (Framo, 1972) to compulsively repeat unresolved conflicts from their own childhoods both in the ways they perceive and the ways they act towards their different children. Children remind us not only of ourselves, but of other people: an abusive spouse, a cherished aunt, a sibling with whom one had been entangled. Children easily come to symbolize the meanings, hopes, and wounds which come with life's relationships.

Family relationships are founded on more than projections. Parental preferences and feelings of affinity hinge on other influences. Was the child wanted at the outset? Children born of unwanted conceptions are less active and responsive in the several days after delivery (Standley, Soule, Copans & Klein, 1978) and they are more accident prone, have poorer health, and face more learning problems than do children who were wanted at conception. Parental "readiness" for child bearing varies from child to child within the family. In one era, the parents may be stressed and unhappy, and a child born at that time may be seen as a burden, while in a more felicitous circumstance the same parents may be prepared to give more to a different child. Estimates based on survey research (Temple University, 1977) suggest that about 15% of all conceptions are consciously unwanted. Clearly, the circumstances of conception and birth need to be understood if favoritism is to be explained.

There are other factors which must be added to the equations we write about favoritism. Children are genetically quite different from one another (Scarr & Grajek, 1982), and they resemble each other only slightly on tests of temperament and personality. In addition, Schachter and her associates (1982) have repeatedly found that parents describe their first and second-born children as being "as different as day and night." These very different children are viewed as resembling different parents, what Schachter calls "split-parent identification." The firstborn is viewed as being like one parent while the other parent and the second-born are perceived as similar in a who-is-like-who division within the family. This emphasis on sibling differences receives even further affirmation in the work of such researchers as Conley (1981), Sears, Maccoby and Levin (1957), and Lasko (1954). Although there are important consistencies in parent's style of interacting with all their children, parents are more anxious with their firstborns; they appear more relaxed and certain of themselves in bringing up children who are born later on (Dunn, 1985). This is fertile soil for favoritism and, its companion, rejection in families. Favoritism may occur in as many as three families out of ten (Ross & Milgram, 1982), and it can be a major factor in the development of life-lasting sibling rivalry.

The case history presented here suggests some of the major dynamics in the development of extreme favoritism, demonstrating a sharply painful family splitting. The strong feelings of love and hate that unite one parent with one child and team them against a second parent and a second child are the result of a confluence of genetic, projective, and social influences that require three generations to develop.

CASE ILLUSTRATION:
FAVORITISM AND REJECTION
ACROSS THREE GENERATIONS

Near the end of psychotherapy which had required more than five years, a fifty-three-year-old woman was referred by her therapist to this writer's research project. She was unusually articulate and emotionally stable at the time of the interview. She was the owner of a small store, middle-class, well educated, divorced for ten years, mother of four grown children who ranged in age from early twenties to early thirties, and herself the eldest of five siblings.

Her children, a girl and three boys, include:

Rebecca: the eldest (dark-eyed, dark hair)

Andy: two years younger (red hair)

Tommy: younger than Andy by 13 months (dark hair)

Jason: two years younger than Tommy (red hair)

The woman is speaking to the interviewer about the birth of her first two children.

Woman: Rebecca's my first born. She was born with just loads of dark hair [the woman leans forward, smiles, glows as she describes], dark eyes, looking very much like her father, I thought. And everything went fine with her.

But Andy was *very* different [her expression becomes serious and unsmiling]. He was a large baby, very large. And the delivery was precipitous. I lost a lot of blood. I nearly died.

And then I remember the moment he was born. Our family doctor, who had known my father for many years, delivered Andy. And I remember him saying: "Oh, my God! He looks exactly like your father!"

Andy's hair was red, very, very red. And when the

doctor told me that, it just sliced right through me.
Here I had this beautiful child, and I didn't even want
to look at him!

The circumstances of birth, whether painful and threatening to
the mother or relatively uncomplicated, set the stage for her attri-
bution of good and bad in her infant. This child's birth nearly
killed the mother; her first experience of a male child was muti-
lating and life-threatening. Pregnancies vary in their ease and
freedom from complications; not only is the mother's attitude
toward the newborn influenced by this encounter but it may influence her newborn's ability to develop normally into an "easy
baby." Some researchers have suggested (Standley et al., 1978),
based on pre-partum interviews with parents, that the general
optimism and energy which the parents bring to childbearing influences the temperament of the infant in the first few days of
life. Cycles of negativity or compatibility in infant and mother
may start early in conception, and these are related to whether the
child was wanted and whether pregnancy and delivery were easy
or difficult.

In this instance, the baby was red-haired (the same color of
hair as the mother and of her own father). Red hair became a
symbol of some upsetting part of this mother's experience with
her own father. Parents react to newborns by searching to see if
the child resembles the mother, the father, the grandfather, the
grandmother. Where there are clear and striking resemblances,
such as hair color, the tendency for parents and other family
members to assign a child to a "good" side or a "bad" side of
the family is enhanced. Yet, the selecting of which trait makes
the parents identify a child as a member of such a group often
appears to be entirely personal. Sometimes hair color or skin
color, obvious markers of difference, are chosen. Whether the
infant is male or female is often charged with deep emotion,
while in other instances, very small variations can be seized
upon, such as a small mole, the shape of the nose, or a gesture,
such as staring, or sneezing, which makes the infant "just like"
his father, uncle, or grandparent. At any rate, physical traits are

only one form of the many infant characteristics that can form a crucial axis for viewing the child as a certain kind of person.

Each parent brings his or her own life's fears and hopes to the delivery room and takes them back to the home in which children develop. Our own experience with acceptance, or rejection influences our acceptance or avoidance of our own children. When the past has been traumatic for one or both of the parents, children become either healing caretakers for the parental wound or aggravating intruders, reminding parents of a pained past that has not been understood. It is a tenet of psychoanalytically-oriented thinking that people repeat compulsively the conflicted aspects of their pasts, and there is no more ample ground on which to enact this than with one's own children.

In the next segment, the woman reveals some of the sources of her own childhood distress. She was bitterly rejected by a mother and favored by a warm, but emotionally abusive father who became her emotional lifeline.

Woman: I was the oldest child. All I can remember was that my mother's next child died when it was just a baby, and she became very depressed; she had no real involvement with me during the early years. I was told she had a nervous breakdown, and she did treat me horribly. She was violent towards me. Things were bizarre because she was much nicer to my sisters. She even pushed me down a flight of stairs. My sisters were on the "inside" and I was on the "outside."

Rejection by one parent can stimulate feelings of affinity with the other parent in a mutual process of finding comfort with each other. Scarr and Grajek (1982) have written that people carve out niches with people they find comfortable and compatible based in part on genetic similarity. The process of rigid splitting off from one parent and finding favor with another parent occurs in desperate family circumstances. "The enemy of my enemy is my friend, and the friend of my enemy is my enemy" wrote Theodore Caplow (1968). The coalition between this woman and her father was based partly on their common anger at the mother, partly on their shared feeling that the mother had abandoned them. It was also based in part on genetic similarities including hair color. None of her siblings had red hair, and only she had the musical aptitudes which her father possessed. To use Scarr's term, this woman and her father became a niche for one another. Genetic resemblance combined uniquely with emotional desperation.

Woman: I always felt close to my father, very close. He was my best buddy. We used to play tennis and bike together. And we were both musical; he taught me all sorts of instruments. He had an absolute passion for music. He shared that with me, that was my refuge, my hiding place. I was the only kid in the second grade who did her homework listening to Tommy Dorsey and Glenn Miller.

I felt loved and comforted by my father, and I suspect that I was closer to him than to anyone else in our family.

The sense that "we are all that one another has" offers an exclusiveness and a sense of understanding, a feeling of being specially loved and understood. It provides a fertile soil for the development of favoritism. Child and parent become each other's favorite person.

Schachter (1982) writes that when one child is viewed by the family as "like the mother," and the other is seen as "like the father," each child may benefit from having attention from one parent. This woman's case, however, illustrates dysfunctional family processes. Here there is no chance for the daughter to get close to the mother; closeness between father and child is fueled by desperation. It is the rigidity of this arrangement and its unalterable nature that makes this family disturbed. Extremes of favoritism and rejection in families such as this appear rigid and insulated from the corrective influences of people outside the family. Therapists were never consulted.

To be a favorite seems life-saving and *is* life-saving for many children. But a singular identification with a parent carries the risk of being subjected to the harmful effects of a parent's emotional problems. Becoming the favorite carries obligations to become an emotional partner with the parent replete with exposure to that parent's immaturities. Paradoxically, favoritism's life-saving aspects can be accompanied by pernicious misuse of a child. A bitter comment made by one favored patient was: "If your parent is disturbed, maybe it's better to be rejected."

The mystery of this woman's rejection of her own first-born male child, Andy, is now clarified through the discovery of the price she paid for her father's exclusive love.

Woman: I've often wondered about my father's love. It saved me and it ruined my life. Even though he preferred me to my sister, he would tell me things I shouldn't know, like the fact that he *had* to get married because mom was pregnant with me. It was: "I love you, and you're my favorite child, but because of you I never accomplished the things I wanted to do."

He drank, and he did some sexually inappropriate things with me when I became 11 years old. I didn't try to stop it until I was older. How could I? He was my everything, and he actually believed I *was* actually him. He would get drunk and look at me and say: "We are alike, you *are* me!"

And there were other questions, like, if he favored me, how could he let my mother abuse me, why didn't he protect me? I was his buddy, but when the chips were down, he somehow couldn't be counted on.

Let us return to the woman's relationship with red-haired Andy, and her reactions to her other children. The present is informed by the past; an unloved infant is "handed over" to a more available parent.

Woman: So I couldn't love that baby. I literally turned Andy over to his father when he was big enough to walk, because I was afraid of what I would do with that child. And, he became his father's shadow. He became his father's favorite.

Because she had no insight into her own childhood trauma, this woman continued to fear producing children who would remind her of the misery of her growing up. Like some parents who have given birth to severely handicapped babies and need to prove they are competent to produce a healthy infant, she needed to conceive a child (her third) who would somehow wash away the ugly, red-haired stain (second-born Andy) of her past life.

Woman: I needed some sort of absolution for producing this child, even though I had been warned it was dangerous to conceive another child for health reasons, but I let myself get pregnant three months later. I literally *prayed* all the way through the pregnancy and all the way through the delivery: "God, please, please make this child a boy, and make this child not look like my father, make him dark haired."

And [proud, triumphant tone] out came just what I wanted, a dark-haired angel, who looked totally unlike my father's side of the family. I was relieved! And, he was such a good baby—an incredible baby. Tommy was as good as gold. He never went through the things that Andy went through.

What came first? Parental expectation and good temperament, or good temperament and the fulfillment of a parental expectation? Family relationships involve the circular interplay of people, making it hard to determine who really started what. This is what makes bridging the research-practice gap so difficult for clinicians, since variables rarely operate singly, and since contexts are all-important. In the next part, we see how context and previous childbearing experience completely changed the meaning of having another red-headed boy. The parent's very personal interpretation of the next birth alters the power of "red-headed" to produce revulsion. Her fourth child, Jason, was born.

Woman: When Jason came out he looked just like Andy, red hair and all.
Interviewer: Same fears, same upset for you?
Woman: [Enthusiastically] Not at all! That little kid sorta said to me: "It's okay."
Interviewer: How was this?
Woman: I guess I was seeing it as part of a pattern. I knew

that I could have some dark-haired kids, and that once in a while there would be a redhead. It seemed inevitable, so it didn't hit me like it did the first time I had a redhead.

And Jason became my most totally favorite child — he almost died when he was born and he needed lots of attention. His father took one look at him and couldn't stand him.

Jason could never win the father's favor as could his older-born, fellow-red-headed brother, Andy. The family became rigidly polarized with parent against parent and child against child.

Woman: If Andy wanted to ride on the truck with his dad, he was welcomed, but if Jason wanted to go, it was always: "Find something else to do."

Families in which extreme favoritism of one child is coupled with extreme rejection of another child are badly divided, as affinities grow and people take sides. Rivalry fueled by the dynamic of favoritism can be severe and life endangering, as each child, siding with an angry parent, plays out his role in a symbolic proxy war (Bank & Kahn, 1982).

Children often enact one parent's contempt for the other parent by attacking the favorite child. It is not uncommon for the aggressor child to go without discipline by the parent with whom he identified and with whom he is allied (Bank & Kahn, 1982; Johnson & Szurek, 1952).

Woman: My husband would blow up, abusively to Jason, but not to Andy. And it seemed that Andy drew all of his personality from his father and Jason got his from me. I was mild and sort of a harmonizer, and this rubbed off on Jason. Andy got his hairtrigger temper from his father and he would take it out on Jason. Andy couldn't stand Jason. For some reason, he seemed to always have a vendetta against him. When Jason was 11, Andy threw a knife at him, and it went right through his arm. His father acted like it was no big deal.

Andy's contempt for Jason grew more extreme with time, and Jason became wary and hostile. Jason, his mother's favorite, both benefitted from her love and nurturing and suffered for it for her attachment to Jason fueled jealousy and bitterness from Andy. Andy, his father's "pride and joy," developed a bitter bond with his mother; bullying his younger brother was another route to his father's esteem for manliness, and it simultaneously allowed him to wreak revenge on his mother for disfavoring him. By the time they became adults, Jason and Andy barely spoke to each other; their relationship was icy and indifferent, defensively masking feelings of fear and rage.

CONCLUSION

Researchers who do not work with patients can benefit from contact with clinicians and with extreme cases such as this one. Clinicians can point to issues of history, emotional context, and family process and point out which aspects of family life seem most crucial. Research on favoritism should involve the study of at least two children and two parents. Although longitudinal study is expensive and difficult, a study of favoritism in a few families during the prenatal months, postnatal period, through the early, mid, late childhood years, and adolescence would clarify the interplay of genetics, social contexts, and family projections. Dunn and Kendrick (1982) have taken a step in this direction by recontacting the young families they initially studied several years earlier. Their results were not only fascinating and rich, but they showed powerful consistencies over time.

Cases such as this one suggest that extreme favoritism leading to unchecked sibling rivalry requires at least one and possibly all of the following factors observed in this case study. They are:

1. Emotional trauma in one or both of the parents during their own childhoods.
2. Conception or birth which is charged with acutely happy or unhappy meanings.
3. Traits in the child (physical, gender-related, intellectual, behavioral) which one or both parents invest with "good" or "bad" meanings.

4. Severe marital conflict accompanied by the inability of the
   family to provide corrections to the "good/bad" identities
   assigned to the children.

Extreme favoritism, coupled as it often is with extreme rejection, is probably statistically infrequent in the general population, but it arises with great frequency in the lives of people who
seek psychotherapy. Moreover, intensive analysis of the extreme
case can often help us understand the ordinary.

When people become adults, it is difficult, and often impossible, to change the course of favoritism. Even the most skilled
therapists find that their efforts to help angry adult siblings
achieve reconciliation will fall flat or will be met with enormous
resistance (for exceptions see Bank & Kahn, 1982; Kahn &
Lewis, 1988). The case presented here convinced this writer that
our energies should be put into early intervention. What might
have occurred had this mother received the support of a nurse or
a preschool teacher who was unafraid to hear her rejection of her
child and who might have mobilized therapeutic help for the family? Would a support group for mothers of "difficult children"
(see Turecki & Toner, 1985) have softened the counterpoint of
favoritism and rejection? Would favoritism so inexorably have
led to rivalry had workers in the health care and educational systems been taught to listen to and act upon this mother's pain?
Those of us who work in the helping professions need to find
ways to hear and to alter parents' deep prejudices before they
become part of the everyday way of being a hurtful family, and
before these prejudices are transmitted to the next generation.

NOTE

1. Which comes first? Parental responsiveness or infant responsiveness to the parent? In all likelihood, a circular model of family influences is needed to account for
parent-child affinity. "Parental responsiveness is only theoretically an antecedent vari-
able. An interpretation in terms of mutual adaptation of mother and infant is likely to do
most justice to the observed facts . . . " (Schaffer & Emerson, 1964). To this we should
add: interpretation requires an understanding, in addition to the mother-infant relationship, of how father-sibling-grandparents, and other significant people provide a context
for development and identity.

REFERENCES

Bank, S. & Kahn, M. D. (1982). *The Sibling Bond*. New York: Basic Books.

Caplow, T. (1986). *Two against one: Coalitions in triads*. Englewood Cliffs, NJ: Prentice Hall.

Conley, J. J. (1981). *Birth order and individual differences in emotional response*. Wesleyan University: Middletown, CT, Department of Psychology.

Dunn, J. (1985). *Sisters and brothers*. Cambridge, MA: Harvard University Press.

Dunn, J. & Kendrick, C. (1982). *Siblings: Love, envy, and understanding*. Cambridge, MA: Harvard University Press.

Framo, J. (1972). Symptoms from a family transactional point of view. In C. Seger & H. S. Kaplan (Eds.), *Progress in group and family therapy*. New York: Brunner/ Mazel.

Johnson, A. M. & Szurek, S. A. (1952). The genesis of antisocial acting-out in children and adults. *Psychoanalytic Quarterly, 21*, 323-343.

Kahn, M. & Lewis, K. (1988). *Siblings in therapy*. New York: W. W. Norton.

Lasko, J. K. (1954). Parent behaviour toward first and second children. *Genetic Psychology Monographs, 49*, 97-137.

Ross, H. G. & Milgram, J. I. (1982). Important variables in adult sibling relationships: A qualitative study. In M. E. Lamb & B. Sutton-Smith (Eds.), *Sibling relationships: Their nature and significance across the life span*. Hillsdale, NJ: Lawrence Erlbaum.

Scarr, S. & Grajek, S. (1982). Similarities and differences among siblings. In M. E. Lamb & B. Sutton-Smith (Eds.), *Sibling relationships: Their nature and significance across the life span*. Hillsdale, NJ: Lawrence Erlbaum.

Schachter, F. F. (1982). Sibling deidentification and split-parent identification. A family tetrad. In M. E. Lamb & B. Sutton-Smith (Eds.), *Sibling relationships: Their nature and significance across the life span*. Hillsdale, NJ: Lawrence Erlbaum.

Schaffer, H. R. & Emerson, P. (1964). The development of social attachments in infancy. *Monographs of the Society for Research in Child Development, 29*, (3).

Sears, R. R., Maccoby, E. & Levin, H. (1957). *Patterns of child rearing*. Evanston, IL: Row, Peterson.

Standley, K., Soule, A. B., Copans, S. A. & Klein, R. P. (1978). Multidimensional sources of infant temperament. *Genetic Psychology Monographs, 98*(2).

Temple University Institute for Survey Research. (1977). *National Survey of Children*. Philadelphia, PA: Author.

Turecki, S. & Tonner, L. (1985). *The difficult child*. New York: Bantam Books.

PART II:
SPECIAL CONCERNS

Siblings and Parents
in One-Parent Families

Edna K. Shapiro, PhD
Doris B. Wallace, PhD

SUMMARY. The number of one-parent households has increased dramatically in recent years, but we know very little about how these families function and even less about sibling relationships in such families. We briefly review earlier research and then describe our work which focuses on siblings and parent in one-parent families who have had time to adapt to their new way of life. Our study is an intensive analysis of six divorced families with one parent at home and a comparison group of seven families with two parents at home; each family has two children. Each family member was interviewed individually and asked comparable questions about family life.

Edna K. Shapiro and Doris B. Wallace are Research Psychologists at Bank Street College, 610 West 112th Street, New York, NY 10025.

This study was supported by the William T. Grant Foundation and Bank Street College. We thank Karen S. Blum for her contribution to interviewing family members and developing measures, and Sarah Hahn Burke for her help with interviewing and data analysis. We thank Howard E. Gruber for his helpful comments on an early draft. Both authors contributed equally to this paper.

We discuss parents' and children's perceptions of the one-parent family, sibling relationships, siblings and parents, and issues specific to threesomes.

Most of what we know about sibling relationships comes from studies of siblings who live with both of their parents. But the enormous increase in one-parent families tells us that we can no longer assume that the typical child one meets and works with lives in a two-parent nuclear family.

What happens when siblings live with one parent? Is their relationship different from that of siblings in two-parent families? Do they compete more intensely for reduced parental resources? Do they draw closer together finding more solidarity and mutual support in their relationship? What happens when the single parent has no other adult with whom to share the daily problems and decisions that parenting involves?

The increasingly large number of one-parent families in our society constitutes both a threat to an existing norm and its replacement by new norms. We need to understand the one-parent family as a different family form, coexisting with the two-parent family, each generating a different constellation of roles and relationships. This will enable us to conceive of the one-parent family, not as the debris remaining after the tidal wave of divorce has ebbed, but as a system with its own adaptive strategies and its own strengths. We know that more and more children are spending a considerable part of their lives with one and not both of their parents. According to Bane (1976), "nearly 40% of the children born around 1970 will . . . live in a one-parent family at some point during their first eighteen years" (p. 14).

The label "single-parent family" covers several kinds of families with quite different histories. It can apply to a family in which one parent has died; to a family headed by a mother who has never married; or to a family whose single-parent status is the result of the dissolution of marriage.

By far, the largest number of single-parent families in this and other Western countries is in the last category, and this kind of family is the one that we are concerned with here. Strictly speaking, these are one-parent households. From the point of view of the children, there may still be two parents in their family, and the absent parent may be quite active in their lives. When we asked children "what makes a family a family," they were quite clear that loving each other, having a conscious bond with other people, caring for each other, and doing things together were the critical ingredients. Thus, living together is not necessarily a criterion for being a family.

PREVIOUS STUDIES: IMPACT OF THE DIVORCE

The rising divorce rate has made divorce a phenomenon in urgent need of attention and understanding, not only because of the human suffering it involves but also because of its important implications for the needs of children and families. Another, more subtle, reason for research interest in the impact of divorce stems from the continued power that the two-parent nuclear family wields as an ideal form and as the continuing authoritative standard in the society. In spite of the divorce statistics, psychologically, the nuclear family, with its intense and long-term relationships among family members, is still considered the social norm, and is the model for most psychological research and theory.

Research on the effects of divorce on children has focused either on short-term effects in the wake of the stress of the separation and divorce or on long-term effects on the children. In either case, there has been very little previous work on the impact of divorce on siblings. We now briefly review the findings on short-term and long-term effects, and then examine the impact of divorce on siblings.

Period Following the Divorce

There is agreement that the period immediately following divorce or separation is one of turmoil and transition that may last two years or more. Hetherington and her associates (Hetherington, Cox & Cox, 1982) and Wallerstein and Kelly (1980) found that children, especially boys who are of preschool age at the time of divorce, appear to be particularly vulnerable and troubled, showing acute separation anxiety and regression at home and school. Is this because boys are generally more vulnerable, or because boys are more likely to lose the same-sex parent and live with the parent of the opposite sex? Or, as Block, Block and Gjerde (1986) suggest, because the boys were more impulsive and undercontrolled before the separation?

Gjerde (1986) has shown that for adolescent children living with both parents, the presence of the father in a mother-child interaction situation enhances the quality of the mother-child relationship, but only for boys. Warshak and Santrock (1983), who have compared the adjustment of children in father- and mother-custody households, have consistently found that outcomes are more problematic for the child who is living with a parent of the opposite sex. But sibling relationships were never studied in these families.

Moving Toward Coping or Continued Mourning

Findings on the long-term effects of divorce on children are inconsistent. Some studies show continued mourning (Wallerstein, 1984), others show only small or no negative effects (e.g., Bernard & Nesbitt, 1981; Kulka & Weingarten, 1979; Kurdek & Siesky, 1980; Reinhard, 1977).

A promising theoretical framework for understanding the long-term effects of divorce on children is offered by Morawetz and Walker (1984) in their useful book about family therapy with single-parent families. They identify four phases in the post-divorce period, at least among families seeking help.

They call the first phase the *aftermath*, a time of intense emotion, confusion, and pain in which children's assumptions about the stability of their world can be deeply shaken. Children may also be extremely anxious about the psychological condition of the parent they live with. Others have noted that it is in this phase that the custodial parent (usually the mother) may temporarily be unable to parent and that young children have fears of abandonment (e.g., Wallerstein & Kelly, 1980). The second phase, *realignment*, is an often stormy period when families accept major undesirable changes, such as a decline in family income, the children's reduced access to both parents, and a changed social life. In the third phase, *reestablishment of social life*, family members adapt to their new status. Children learn to live without one parent, or to move between two households, the parents learn to negotiate with each other as parents, or to get along without each other, and the future does not look so bleak. Finally, in the fourth phase, *separation*, "parent and child separate as the child moves off into a life of his own, confident that the parent has his own life in hand and can manage without the child" (Morawetz & Walker, 1984, p. 27). It can be seen that Morawetz and Walker see these families as following a general developmental course towards coping and adaptation.

Siblings in Divorced Families

In general, most formal, statistical studies of one-parent families or of the impact of divorce select a single "target" child in a family and compare him or her with a child of the same age and sex in an intact family. It is easy to see that such a research design makes it impossible to study the impact of divorce on siblings as only one child in the family is selected.

Other studies, based on interviews with parents or children in one-parent families, have yielded some interesting observations about siblings, even though here too the siblings themselves have not been the object of study. Springer and Wallerstein (1983) interviewed 14 adolescents, 12 to 14 years old, each from a different family, whose parents had recently separated or divorced. All but one had siblings, and the authors conclude that their relationships with their siblings "became more meaningful after the marital separation, and . . . appeared to be significant sources of conflict and competitiveness, as well as of security and continuity" (p. 21). Polit (1984) interviewed single mothers of one, two or three children and found that "virtually all" the mothers of more than one child reported sibling squabbles, although few attributed this to their single-parent situation. Weiss (1979a, 1979b) also interviewed parents who were bringing up children on their own. He notes that there may be increased rivalry between siblings for the single parent's love and affection because "the stock of parental investment has been reduced," but also that siblings may become more important to each other as potential allies and confidants.

Although these findings are provocative, none of the studies focused on the sibling relationship itself and in none of these studies were all the children in the family interviewed. Recent research on siblings as well as clinically based theory indicate that a broader approach to studying the effects of family disruption on siblings is needed, namely one that sees the family as a system. Recent sibling studies suggest that children in the same family may not have the same reaction to the separation and divorce. Daniels and Plomin (1985) have shown that siblings can perceive the social and affective aspects of their family environment in very different ways and experience different treatment from their parents. Furthermore, there is evidence that mothers tend to perceive members of sibling dyads in contrasting ways, as do the siblings themselves (Schachter, 1982; Schachter, Shore, Feldman-Rotman, Marquis & Campbell, 1976). Findings such as these call for a systems approach to understanding the impact of divorce on siblings. Research and theory in family therapy (e.g., S. Minuchin, 1974) also point up the need to examine relationships in context, for example, how sibling relationships are affected by parent-child relationships.

In the present study, we adopt a systems approach to studying the family. Because systemic issues are, by their nature, complex and because a systems approach has not been applied in research on the impact of family breakup on siblings, an exploratory, intensive study of a small group of families seemed more appropriate than a large-scale statistical study. Intensive analysis can illuminate significant systemic issues, important to the practitioner and helpful as a guide to future research.

Two main methodological considerations guided our approach: (a) we focused on daily life in the restabilized one-parent family so as to be able to examine how the family system operates once the period of acute stress following the separation is over; and (b) we collected data from all members of the household.

SIBLING RELATIONSHIPS IN
ONE- AND TWO-PARENT FAMILIES

Our aim was to examine sibling and other family relationships in one-parent families and to compare these with relationships in two-parent families.

There were 13 families in the study, 5 with one parent (4

mother- and one father-headed), one family in which custody was shared, and 7 with two parents. Altogether, 26 children and 21 parents were interviewed.[1]

The families are urban, white, educated, and financially above average. Nearly all the parents were in their thirties and forties and had been married for a long time.[2] For those who divorced, the period since the breakup of the marriage ranged from 3 to 10 years with an average of 6.5 years. We chose families that were not under financial stress, and focused on the period beyond the painful post-separation phases because we wanted to study one-parent families that had an opportunity to develop positive strategies for coping with their new family situation. Each family had two children of the same gender between the ages of 8 and 17, who were between 18 months and 4 years apart. We chose to study children of this age because they can articulate their ideas and feelings. Same-sex siblings were chosen to control for gender effects while studying sibling effects. Since other research indicates that boys and girls react differently to divorce, it seemed wise to conduct this exploratory study on same-sex siblings only.

Parents and children were individually interviewed and were asked comparable questions about family life. The interview included factual and open-ended questions, rating scales, and checklists. The questions dealt with the sibling relationship, family members' roles, judgments about family relationships, indices of life satisfaction and stress as well as other aspects of family life not dealt with here. Members of one-parent families were asked a subset of questions about relationships with the noncustodial parent, and the impact of the separation on the parents and their children. All family members were asked to give their perceptions of their roles and relationships with other family members, as well as their view of the roles and relationships of others in the family. The advantage of this method is that it provides information from each family member which goes beyond the sum of its parts and makes it possible to identify patterns of agreement and disagreement in the family as a whole.

It is important to make clear at the outset that we wished to identify successful coping strategies as well as problems in the one-parent family and in the sibling relationship. When we began our study, most developmental and clinical theory about siblings was concerned with rivalry and competition or with the relative merits of being born first or later, and most of the work about the one-parent family focused on it as a broken two-parent family. Fortunately, a new trend has begun to emerge in research on siblings which does not focus only on conflict in the relationship (see Dunn, 1983; Dunn & Kendrick, 1982; Lamb & Sutton-Smith, 1982). Most studies of the one-parent family, however, are still concerned with its disadvantage and its status as a family at risk, as Morawetz and Walker (1984) also note.

Because our study and its method were based on the conception of the family as a system of relationships, in this paper, we do not examine the sibling relationship as an isolated dyad but as part of a network of family relationships. Accordingly, we first report parents' and children's perceptions of being in a one-parent family. We then present perceptions of the sibling relationship, and the relationships of children and parents, with special focus on relationship patterns in the one-parent family. Finally, we discuss our findings and the issues raised by the study.

Children's Perceptions of Being in a One-Parent Family

When asked whether they thought a two-parent or a one-parent family was better, the children had varied and often mixed reactions. Some of the children in one-parent families said that living in a one-parent family gave them more freedom and was less regimented. One 16-year-old girl who had been living with her father and sister for three years said:

> It depends if you're in a family that's happy. My friend is an only child and her parents are staying together for her sake. I think that's sort of nerve wracking. I'd rather have two separate, sane parents.

An older brother pointed to advantages in material things. "You get two of everything: two Christmases, two birthdays . . . " On the other hand, a 14-year-old girl singled out Christmas as a "hard time because you have memories of when everybody was there." On the positive side, she made this comment about her friends who also lived with one parent: "They're closer to their parents because instead of their parents talking to each other, they talk to their children." This comment was borne out by our data.

Some of the younger children would clearly prefer having both parents at home, or expressed mixed sentiments. In another vein, a 12-year old who was 18 months old at the time of separation counted herself lucky to have no actual memories of her former two-parent household.

Different Responses to the Separation

When asked whether the loss of one parent had been harder for one or the other of their children, almost all single parents spoke of the differences in each child's reactions. The characteristics that they talked about as making a difference are exactly what one might expect, the child's age at the time of separation, differences in temperament, and the nature of the pre-separation relationship with the parent with whom they no longer live.

One mother, who thought the separation had taken a tremendous toll on both her children, believed it had been hard for them in different ways. Jeff,[3] the older boy,

> was hard hit because he was the older and was more responsible for the tenor of things in the family, and because he has trouble talking about his feelings. On the other hand, he had friends and was established in the community . . . It hit Teddy at a time when he and his father had a very close relationship and he was young enough so he didn't understand at all. But because he is better able to express his feelings, he got it out of his system and has been able to go out in the world and cope better [than Jeff].

In another family, the younger daughter had had an especially close relationship with her father. As she described it, "Dad and I, before he moved out, I never left his side; I think I liked Dad a lot more than Mom did . . . " Her older sister, Ella said, "I've had a better time with my father and I think my father and I have gotten much closer [since he moved out]." And the mother said: "Ella gained a father." The younger daughter, however, made it clear that she had suffered a loss.

Perceived Satisfaction

All of the children were asked to place themselves on a line from "Here's a person who thinks she's/he's got a pretty good life, thinks she's/he's pretty lucky" to " . . . wishes some of the things in her/his life were different, thinks other kids are luckier." The children in one-parent families, like those in two-parent families, placed themselves close to or at the positive end of the scale.

Parents' Perception of Being in a One-Parent Family

The parents in both groups were asked how they felt about how their lives were going. Only two parents, both married mothers, expressed dissatisfaction with their lives. The most positive responses came from the single-parent mothers.

We asked the single parents about the satisfactions and dissatisfactions of being a single parent, how their relationship with their children had changed since their separation from their ex-spouse, and about the advantages and disadvantages for the children of living in a one-parent household.

Single parents expressed some of the difficulties of "going it alone": the lack of intimacy with another adult, the lack of personal freedom and the negative consequences for the children of family disruption and of having no adult male in the household. But they expressed great satisfaction about their personal development, and liked being the sole adult authority in the family. They were unanimous in their belief that their relationship with their children had become closer and that there was more sharing with the children. When asked if the children are a support to them, the single mothers were more enthusiastically affirmative than the married parents. Parents and children in one-parent families also reported that they confide in and consult each other in making large and small decisions more than was reported by those in two-parent families. Weiss (1979b) has pointed out that since the parent in the one-parent family does not have the other parent to consult, the hierarchic authority structure of the two-parent family crumbles. The parent is more apt to consult with the children, and to draw them into making decisions about family life and family rules. This was certainly borne out in our interviews. Generally, there seems to be a richer connection between children and parent in one-parent families, one that is less bound by the generational hierarchy than in the two-parent families.

In general, then, those parents and children who had been living in one-parent households for several years were not discontented with their situation. Almost without exception, the single parents were proud of having come through a bad time successfully. While some of them were lonely for adult companionship, and some were concerned about their children, they also dwelt on the close relationship they had with their children and the pleasure this gave them. In the two-parent families, such feelings were less of a feature and were, perhaps, taken more for granted. The children in one-parent families thought they had a pretty good life and few of them saw the one-parent family in a negative light. We do not want to overinterpret this, but it does fit the objective facts and the children's general demeanor. These children were not miserable or depressed; they were healthy, affluent, well cared for; they had friends. A number of the children were sad when they talked about their parents' separation; and a few believed there are great advantages in living with both parents, and perhaps long for parental reconciliation. At the same time, the general impression that the parents and children gave is of successful coping.

Perceptions of Sibling Relationships

What did children and parents say about the sibling relationship? How did siblings describe each other? Did they think that there are more advantages or more disadvantages in having a sister or a brother? Did they think being an only child was better or worse?

Different Perceptions of Parents and Children

When asked to describe their relationship on a series of rating scales, from close to distant, helpful to not helpful, loving to not loving, the children's mean ratings and those of the parents in both one- and two-parent families were all on the positive side (see Figures 1a and 1b). Children, and especially parents, also believe that the siblings openly express their feelings toward each other, that the relationship is not always easygoing, and that it is stormy rather than calm. In effect, the sibling relationship is viewed as one that accommodates desirable qualities as well as tensions and conflicts.

The differences between the ratings of children in one- and two-parent families are negligible (see Figure 1a), except that children in one-parent families rate their relationship as somewhat less close and loving than do children in two-parent families. Differences between single and married parents are simi-

FIGURE 1a

a. CHILDREN'S PERCEPTIONS

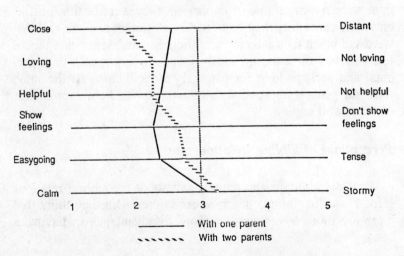

FIGURE 1b

b. PARENTS' PERCEPTIONS

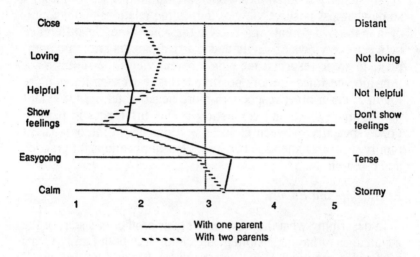

———— With one parent
˷˷˷˷˷˷ With two parents

larly small (see Figure 1b), although the single mothers view their children's relationship as more loving and also more tense than do the married parents. More striking are the different perceptions of the children and parents in one-parent families (see solid lines in Figures 1a and 1b).

The roles that the siblings are seen to take with each other follow a somewhat similar pattern (see Figures 2a and 2b). All believe that the children are friends and that they comfort and teach each other (though older siblings far more often than younger take the role of teacher). Parents and children in both kinds of families also see the children as competing with and teasing each other. Again, the sibling relationship is viewed as encompassing both positive and negative roles and there are few differences between one- and two-parent families. Children in one-parent families, however, although they see themselves as teachers, friends and comforters just as often as do children in two-parent families, are more likely to view themselves as competitors and teasers (see Figure 2a). Single and married parents, on the other hand, show only negligible differences in their perceptions of the incidence of these sibling roles (see Figure 2b). Thus, as before, there are differences between the perceptions of children and parents, this time in both kinds of families.

Altogether, children in the one-parent families seem to hold a somewhat less positive view of the sibling relationship than children in the two-parent families. On the other hand, the difference between the views of single and married parents are more complex. In some respects, the single parent views the sibling relationship and roles in more positive terms, for example, as more loving, and in other respects in more negative terms, for example, as more tense and competitive. The differences in perception, especially between children and parents in the one-parent family, warrants attention because it has implications for practice and research.

Friendship and Enmity

In describing what they like about their brother or sister, or the advantages of having a sibling, the children in both family forms repeatedly mentioned qualities such as "sticks up for me," "comforts me," "helps me," "talks to me like I'm a friend."

FIGURE 2a

a. CHILDREN'S PERCEPTIONS

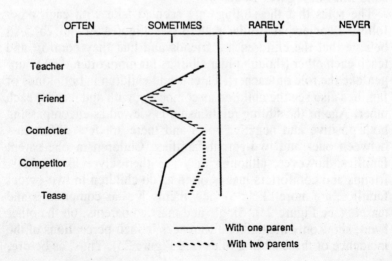

FIGURE 2b

b. PARENTS' PERCEPTIONS

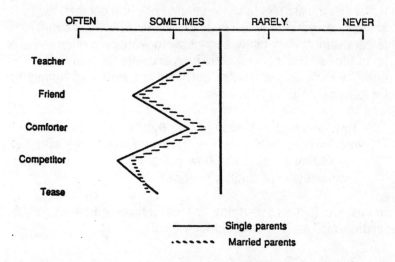

- ———— Single parents
- .... Married parents

Some expressed a sense of deep indebtedness to their sibling, for example, "I've got almost everything from her, she developed my personality," "without her I would be very unhappy."

Coexisting with these deep positive feelings, there was often intense animosity expressed in quarreling, teasing, and mutual torment. This was especially evident among brothers who more often described getting into physical fights with each other. One boy, when asked what his younger brother is like, responded, "He's insufferable" and went on to describe how. There is considerable support in the literature for the idea that boys are more openly aggressive than girls (Parke & Slaby, 1983), but boys can get along and be "true friends" as one single mother put it. She described how her older son included his younger brother in games with his friends. The younger brother in this family said, "He's really nice to me, like when my mom gets mad at me, Jeff would help me, and try to stop me from crying"; or responding to a question about how you show your affection, he said, "I try to be nice, and if he wants to play a certain game, I say yes, even if I don't want to." Of course, they do fight, according to Jeff, "just sometimes, when we go too far in teasing. If he tells secrets, that usually starts a fight, but Mom knows I won't hit him hard because we like each other so much."

While girls are less likely to get into physical combat, they can be very competitive. One single mother described her daughters' relationship: "They really know how to work each other over. A lot of the bad feeling is essentially over competition for my affection," which, as she pointed out, is also a matter of competing for her time. She went on to say:

> I'm interested in how much the fighting is a punishment of me for being a bad mother and how much in the nature of the sibling relation and how much it's their *very* different temperaments. I think it's all of them.

In this, she tells us something that researchers sometimes forget, relationships are seldom unidimensional.

The Thought of Being an Only Child

Altogether, almost three-quarters of all children said it was better to have a sibling than to be an only child and among children living in one-parent families, two-thirds were of this opinion: "It's nice to have a brother to talk to and play with," "I'd be lonely and bored." Some were ambivalent: "It would be worse on the whole [to be an only child], but you wouldn't have so many fights."

Being Different

In the sample as a whole, more children considered themselves different from rather than like their sibling (58% to 27%), while a smaller proportion (15%) saw a mix of similarity and difference. Boys more often than girls said they were different (75% to 43%). This trend cuts across one-parent and two-parent homes: two-thirds of the siblings in one-parent families and half of those in two-parent families emphasized the differences rather than the similarities. The younger members of sibling pairs were somewhat more likely to see themselves as different (69% to 46%).

These trends are in agreement with Schachter's (1982; Schachter, Shore, Feldman-Rotman, Marquis & Campbell, 1976) findings that siblings, especially the first pair and especially siblings of the same sex, are more apt to see themselves as different than as similar, a phenomenon Schachter has called *deidentification*. Each sibling carves out a niche for herself or himself that is different from the sister's or brother's. Schachter hypothesizes that deidentification is a defense against sibling rivalry. It may mitigate rivalry but note also that in our sample these judgments of difference go hand in hand with accounts of rivalry and bickering.

Relationships of Siblings and Parents

We have already noted that all of the parents who were living apart from their ex-spouses described their present relationships with their children as much closer than before the marital breakup. Parents in two-parent families also spoke of family closeness, but it had a different quality.

Support

While married mothers are among those who referred to their children as an emotional support, their responses, like those of their husbands, imply a distance or hierarchy: "They are companions on their level," "When I'm sad they bring me fruit." The single mothers' responses were more intense and enthusiastic, and included a view of the children as people rather than only as children. For example, they said, "Absolutely, in emotional ways . . . just being here, they are good to come home to, it's a wonderful family, I can talk to them," " . . . they occupy your thoughts and give you a reason for working hard, and their love of you is a support."

It is as if, for the married parents, children are a support just by existing, or by doing something special when the occasion warrants it. The single parents, on the other hand, convey that the support which they derive from their children is in the nature of the relationship they have with their children as people, less governed by the parent-child hierarchy than in the two-parent families.

The children, too, expressed their closeness to their parents, especially to their mothers. The mother was definitely the person they felt closer to, especially children living with one parent (75% by contrast to 36% of children in two-parent families). When asked: "Who in the family knows you best," 83% said their mother (as opposed to 36% of children in two-parent families). Further, only one child from a one-parent family who said his mother knows him best mentioned anyone else; whereas, most of those from two-parent families also mentioned someone else. The mother was also the preferred person to go to with problems, but family composition does not make a difference here: 64% of the children in one-parent and 71% of those in two-parent households said they went to their mother when something was bothering them, and when they were in trouble. Since we are particularly interested in sibling relationships, we should note that siblings were not often mentioned spontaneously as supportive figures, and when they were, it was younger siblings who spoke of going to their older sibling for support; older siblings tended to go to their friends.

Fathers

Fathers were rarely mentioned as supports by the children. For example, no child in the study mentioned the father first as someone to whom one goes with problems, and only two children (one girl, one boy) said the father was the person who knows her/him best. The mother is clearly the salient support figure, and especially so in the one-parent households.

One interesting aspect of life in these one-parent families is that the children generally did not talk to one parent about the other. In the interviews with two-parent families, this topic did not arise. In the one-parent family, there are issues of loyalty, and of protecting the child-parent relationships from getting involved with, or tainted by, the distant or hostile relationship between the parents. This makes discussion of one parent with the other almost a taboo topic. Several of the single parents told us that they make it a principle not to discuss their ex-spouse with their children. This means that the children are likely to have more information about each parent than either of the parents do. What are the implications of such a situation?

Threesomes

The pattern of intimacy and closeness described by the single parents and many of their children is not always so generally loving and cozy. In all the one-parent families we interviewed, the parents described very different relationships with each of their children. In several families, the potential for the threesome to break into a two-versus-one situation was realized. Alliances were consistently between the mother and the older child. In three one-parent families, the younger child was clearly the odd one out. Two of these mothers also thought that the younger had been shortchanged in the early years before the separation.

One mother, for example, spoke of the advantages that her older son had that the younger one did not have. Even before the breakup of the marriage, she was not able to give Charles, the younger, the kind of care, attention, and nurturing that Robert had because she was depressed and "having a hard time coping" during the first few years of Charles' life. She now depends on Robert more, and he has a more responsible role in the family:

> When I need something done like changing a light switch, in truth both kids can do it, as Charles has pointed out to me, but I'll ask Robert. When I want something done that men do, I'll turn to Robert just because he's older.

Robert, 16 years old, enjoys his power in the family. His status is enhanced by the fact that he has a better relationship with his father than his younger brother. Robert and his father are more alike, and also Robert has excelled in school which has been very important to his father. Charles, on the other hand, has not done well in school, which has been a source of trouble with his father and a bone of contention between the parents (the father thinks his former wife should have pushed Charles more). Here too, Robert has taken an authoritative role and tried to help Charles by encouraging him to do his schoolwork. Charles said that on some of the weekends with his father, his father spends the whole time "bugging" him about his school work. Although he feels closer to his mother and said his mother knows him best, he also said that there is no one who knows him the way he really is. While Charles is often the focus of disapproving attention, he feels himself to be the odd man out in the family.

In two other one-parent families, the mother and older daughter are very intimate. In both families, while the younger daughter was not completely shut out, she seemed somewhat of a second-class citizen. In one of these families, the younger daughter said she does not go into her mother's room if her sister and mother are talking. Both of these younger daughters described their relationship with their sister and mother as less close than the older sister and mother did.

The danger that the single parent, especially the mother, may place too much responsibility on one of the children, usually the older, has been described in the clinical literature as the exploitation of the "parental child" role (e.g., Weltner, 1982). On the other hand, these are not pathological families and responsibility is not necessarily undesirable. In the three families where the mother had forged a special bond with her oldest child, she had not abdicated her parental role nor had the older sibling become a surrogate parent. Rather, the mother had enlisted the older sibling into becoming a quasi peer. The older child had accepted this role and this had led to an increasingly intimate familiarity with the mother's private life. The younger child was not included in this intimacy. Such alliances are probably not exclusive to one-parent families, but the two-parent two-child family permits parent-child alliances that allow each member of the family to have someone with whom to have a special relationship, with no one left out (see for example, Schachter [1982]).

Clinicians, especially family therapists (S. Minuchin, 1974), for a long time have been familiar with such alliances and the impact they can have on relationships within the family. What is needed now is a systematic and fine-grained study of such relationship patterns and the different forms they take in one- and two-parent families and in families of different sizes. This would have the additional advantage of bridging clinical knowledge, practice, and social science research (see P. Minuchin, 1985).

DISCUSSION AND IMPLICATIONS FOR PRACTICE

These findings shed light on family life in the one-parent family and point up the importance of a systems approach to research and practice with families.

First, there is the consistent finding that members of the same family have different perceptions of family experiences including the breakup itself and its impact on family relationships. In the one-parent families, mothers almost uniformly reported that their two children reacted differently to the divorce. The siblings, in turn, view themselves as different rather than alike. Further, mothers and children in one-parent families have different perceptions of the sibling relationship.

These differences in perception may help to account for the contradictory findings in the research literature on the long-term impact of divorce (Block, Block & Gjerde, 1986). They are supported by other studies (Barnes & Olson, 1985; Daniels & Plomin, 1985; Larson, 1974; Safilios-Rothschild, 1970) and have important implications for clinicians and educators working with members of one-parent families. The varying perceptions of different family members highlight the risk of relying on one family member as the informant for the whole family, as in most previous research, and point up the need to collect information from as many family members as possible, including all siblings.

Secondly, these findings indicate that family dynamics in the one-parent family differ from those in the two-parent family in that single parents seem to become closer to their children than married parents do. This closer relationship may be a compensation for the literally more distant relationship with the absent parent, and may serve as a buffer for the stresses of family breakup (e.g., Felner, 1984). Practitioners should be aware of this important buffering role of the parent-child relationship and carefully evaluate its quality. The risk of over intimacy also needs to be considered, since such attachment between parent and child, like excessive distance, can have negative effects.

Thirdly, the three-member family of one-parent two-siblings is different from the four-member two-parents and two-siblings family. Family therapists have described family triangles in which one parent may be allied with one child against the other parent. In the threesome, the single parent may ally with one sibling, leaving the other sibling as an outsider. The dynamics of the threesome also underlines our point that studies of the long-term impact of divorce on children (with their inconsistent findings), have tended to include only one child in the family, neglecting the fact that siblings often play different roles in the family. We are still at the beginning of the effort to describe and understand sibling relationships at different stages of development and in different contexts. Research that sees the family as an organized system of intimate relationships is sorely needed.

In general, our emphasis has been on coping strategies of the one-parent families. At the same time, children who live with one parent face difficult relationship issues for which they often are not prepared either developmentally or because there are no precedents or models, and no resources. We should not overlook the sadness, nostalgia, and tears. But that is not all there is. Although they have suffered, parents and children have good things to say about themselves and their families. They do not perceive life in general, or life in a one-parent family, as disadvantaged. They have come through.

NOTES

1. The sex of the children were as follows:

	Two-parent	One-parent	Shared custody
sisters	4	3	—
brothers	3	2	1

The boys in the shared custody family moved from one parent to the other every three or four days. They spent much more time with each parent than the other children in one-parent households who were typically seeing their noncustodial parent every other weekend.

We had hoped to include more single fathers but this proved extremely difficult since in such families the children either were too young to be interviewed or the custodial father was reluctant to participate. Conversations with potential participants and observation of meetings of single-parent men (who are a small minority of the single-parent population) suggest that, for fathers, the single-parent role was so new that participation in a study such as ours would have been too threatening.

2. The parents' ages ranged from 35 to 51, with a mean of 43.5 years. Those in two-parent families had been married for an average of 17 years, and those in the one-parent families for an average of 12 years. For all these parents, this is or was the first marriage.

The average family income is approximately $55,000 for the group as a whole, and $40,000 for the one-parent families. (All the single parents are employed and all but two of the two-parent families are dual career families.) The one-parent households all receive supplementary funds from the ex-spouse or other family members. Although the difference in income between the one- and two-parent households is considerable, all of the families' incomes place them solidly in the middle or upper-middle class. Some of the one-parent families had earlier experienced great economic stress, but their situation had improved, usually as a result of career advances by one or both parents.

3. All names used in this paper are fictitious.

REFERENCES

Bane, M. J. (1976). *Here to stay: American families in the twentieth century.* New York: Basic.

Barnes, H. L., & Olson, D. H. (1985). Parent-adolescent communication and the circumplex model. *Child Development, 56,* 438-447.

Bernard, J. M., & Nesbitt, S. (1981). Divorce: An unreliable predictor of children's emotional predispositions. *Journal of Divorce, 4,* 31-40.

Block, J. H., Block, J., & Gjerde, P. F. (1986). The personality of children prior to divorce: A prospective study. *Child Development, 57,* 827-840.

Daniels, D., & Plomin, R. (1985). Differential experience of siblings in the same family. *Developmental Psychology, 21,* 747-760.

Dunn, J. (1983). Sibling relationships in early childhood. *Child Development, 54,* 787-811.

Dunn, J., & Kendrick, C. (1982). *Siblings: Love, envy and understanding.* Cambridge, MA: Harvard University Press.

Felner, R. D. (1984). Vulnerability in childhood. In M. C. Roberts & L. Peterson (Eds.), *Prevention of problems in childhood.* New York: Wiley.

Gjerde, P. F. (1986). The interpersonal structure of family interaction settings: Parent-adolescent relations in dyads and triads. *Developmental Psychology, 22,* 297-304.

Hetherington, E. M., Cox, M., & Cox, R. (1982). Effects of divorce on parents and children. In M. E. Lamb (Ed.), *Nontraditional families.* Hillsdale, NJ: Erlbaum.

Kulka, R. A., & Weingarten, H. (1979). The long-term effects of parental divorce in childhood on adult adjustment. *Journal of Social Issues, 4,* 50-78.

Kurdek, L. A., & Siesky, A. E. (1980). Effects of divorce on children: The relationship between parent and child perspectives. *Journal of Divorce, 2,* 85-93.

Lamb, M. E., & Sutton-Smith, B. (1982). *Sibling relationships: Their nature and significance across the lifespan.* Hillsdale, NJ: Erlbaum.

Larson, L. E. (1974). System and subsystem perception of family roles. *Journal of Marriage and The Family, 36,* 123-138.

Minuchin, P. (1985). Families and individual development: Provocations from the field of family therapy. *Child Development, 56,* 289-302.

Minuchin, S. (1974). *Families and family therapy.* Cambridge, MA: Harvard University Press.

Morawetz, A., & Walker, G. (1984). *Brief therapy with single-parent families.* New York: Bruner/Mazel.

Parke, R. D., & Slaby, R. G. (1983). The development of aggression. In E. M. Hetherington (Ed.), *Socialization, personality and social development* (Vol. IV), of P. Mussen (Ed.), *Handbook of child psychology* (4th ed.). New York: Wiley.

Polit, D. (1984). The only child in single-parent families. In T. Falbo (Ed.), *The single-child family.* New York: Guilford.

Reinhard, D. W. (1977). The reaction of adolescent boys and girls to the divorce of their parents. *Journal of Clinical Child Psychology, 2,* 21-23.

Safilios-Rothschild, C. (1970). Family sociology or wives' family sociology? A cross-cultural examination of decision-making. *Journal of Marriage and the Family, 31,* 290-301.

Schachter, F. F. (1982). Sibling deidentification and split-parent identification: A family tetrad. In M. E. Lamb & B. Sutton-Smith (Eds.), *Sibling relationships: Their nature and significance across the lifespan.* Hillsdale, NJ: Erlbaum.

Schachter, F. F., Shore, E., Feldman-Rotman, S., Marquis, R. E., & Campbell, S. (1976). Sibling deidentification. *Developmental Psychology, 12,* 418-427.

Springer, C., & Wallerstein, J. S. (1983). Young adolescents' responses to their parents' divorces. In L. A. Kurdek (Ed.), *Children and divorce,* New Directions in Child Development, No. 19.

Wallerstein, J. S. (1984). Children of divorce: Preliminary report of a ten-year follow-up of young children. *American Journal of Orthopsychiatry, 54,* 444-458.

Wallerstein, J. S., & Kelly, J. B. (1980). *Surviving the breakup: How children and parents cope with divorce.* New York: Basic.

Warshak, R. A., & Santrock, J. W. (1983). The impact of divorce in father-custody and mother-custody homes: The child's perspective. In L. A. Kurdek (Ed.), *Children and divorce.* New Directions in Child Development, No. 19.

Weiss, R. S. (1979a). *Going it alone.* New York: Basic.

Weiss, R. S. (1979b). Growing up a little faster: The experience of growing up in a single-parent household. *Journal of Social Issues, 35,* 97-111.

Weltner, J. S. (1982). A structural approach to the single-parent family. *Family Process, 21,* 203-210.

Siblings and Mental Illness: Heredity vs. Environment

David C. Rowe, PhD
Patricia Elam

SUMMARY. Contemporary behavior genetics has found that siblings are far more likely to be different than alike in personality and in psychopathology. To understand these sibling differences, the dichotomy of heredity and environment needs to be replaced by a four-fold distinction between genetic and environmental factors that are shared by siblings and those which siblings do not share in common. Different genes and different environmental experiences can account for why one sibling becomes mentally ill and another is not affected. Environmental experiences that are unique to each sibling play a much more important role than has been recognized heretofore.

John Wideman and his brother Robert grew up in the same home, but John became a university professor and prize-winning novelist, whereas his brother Robert was sentenced to prison for murder (Wideman, 1984). How could siblings who usually share many of the same genes and many of the same environmental experiences take such different courses in life? In fact, although the Wideman brothers are an extreme case, they serve to illustrate one of the most interesting findings of contemporary behavior genetics, namely, that siblings are far more likely to be different than alike in personality and in psychopathology.

In the realm of psychopathology, sibling similarity is expressed in terms of the risk of siblings acquiring the same mental illness. Risk estimates are based on family, twin, and adoption

David C. Rowe is Associate Professor, University of Oklahoma, Norman, OK 73019; Patricia Elam is a candidate for the PhD at the University of Oklahoma.

studies showing the percent of family members with the same psychiatric diagnosis. Overall, these studies have found that the risk of developing the same mental illness as that of one's sibling is low.

More specifically, Rowe and Plomin (1981) estimate that the risk for siblings of the mentally ill ranges from 10% to 20%. These estimates are based largely on studies of adult schizophrenia and manic-depressive psychosis. There are far fewer studies of the psychiatric (DSM-III) disorders of childhood, but the evidence that is available also shows a low risk for siblings (Graham & Stevensen, 1985; Ritvo, Freeman, Mason-Brothergs, Mo & Ritvo, 1985; Twito & Stewart, 1985; Welner, Welner, Stewart, Palkes & Wish, 1977). For example, for aggressive conduct disorder, Twito and Stewart (1985) find the risk to be only 20.5% for male siblings and 8.8% for female.

These are very reassuring findings. This means that in the typical two-child American family, when one child is mentally ill, the other child is not likely to suffer from the same illness. As we shall see, this reassurance needs to be qualified by what we have learned of the role of heredity in some kinds of mental illness.

GENES: SHARED AND NOT SHARED BY SIBLINGS

Do low risks for siblings mean that heredity or the genes play no role in determining whether the child acquires the behavior disorder of the sibling? No, heredity can account for sibling differences as well as sibling similarities. As illustrated in Table 1, there are genes that siblings share in common which can account for similarities between them, and genes that they do not share in common which can account for differences. Similarly, Table 1 shows that there are environmental influences that siblings share in common which lead to their similarity, and environmental influences that they do not share which lead to sibling differences. To understand the role of heredity and environment in determining whether or not a child will acquire the same disorder as his/her sibling, we need to replace the familiar dichotomy of heredity and environment with a new four-fold distinction between genetic and environmental factors that are shared by siblings and those that are not shared, as shown in Table 1.

Table 1

Four-fold Classification of Genetic and Environmental Influences

Influences	
Genetic	Environmental
Shared by siblings	Shared by siblings
Not shared by siblings	Not shared by siblings

On an average, siblings share about 50% of their genes, but the other 50% of their genes are different. Some siblings share a much smaller percentage of their genes; others share a much larger percentage which accounts for the average of 50%. The shared genes might account for why two siblings suffer from the same mental illness (i.e., when both share the gene(s) for the illness), while the nonshared genes might account for why one sibling is affected and the other is not (i.e., when one has the gene(s) for the illness and the other does not).

If genes can account for both sibling similarity and dissimilarity in psychopathology, we cannot learn whether heredity plays a role in the development of a given mental illness simply by examining the degree of overall risk for siblings. It requires, therefore, the comparison of risks among people who are more or less genetically similar (e.g., identical twins vs. fraternal twins, biological siblings vs. adoptive ones, or family members vs. nonrelatives). Taking the example of adult schizophrenia, identical twins are more than twice as likely to share this mental illness as are fraternal twins (Rowe & Plomin, 1981). Since the identicals share more genes than the fraternals (100% vs. an average of 50%) and they are the ones most likely to share the same psychopathology, it is safe to conclude that genes play a role in the development of adult schizophrenia.

Is there evidence that heredity plays a role in the development of childhood psychology? There is more evidence of genetic influence for *externalizing disorders*, in which the child's behavior is undercontrolled and disruptive to others, than there is for *inter-*

nalizing disorders such as problems of anxiety, in which the child is typically over-controlled. Among the externalizing disorders showing evidence of increased risks to family members, including siblings, are: (a) attention deficit disorder (formerly, hyperactivity, Cantwell, 1975; Morrison & Stewart, 1973; Safer, 1973; Welner et al., 1977), (b) aggressive conduct disorder (Jary & Stewart, 1985; Twito & Stewart, 1982), and (c) juvenile delinquency (Rowe & Osgood, 1984). By contrast, there is a lacunae of knowledge concerning the patterns of familial aggregation for the internalizing problems such as anxiety disorders. Finally, one twin study of infantile autism provides evidence of increased risks to siblings (Ritvo et al., 1985).

Thus, the conclusion that children are not likely to acquire the mental illness of their siblings needs to be qualified. In absolute terms, the risk for siblings is low for all mental illness. On the other hand, in relative terms, the risk for siblings appears to be higher than for unrelated children in the case of externalizing disorders and autism. Genes alone, however, do not account for the development of psychopathology in children. Environmental factors also play a crucial role. In fact, based on twin and adoption studies, behavior geneticists conclude that heredity and environment play roughly equal roles in the development of personality and psychopathology (Rowe & Plomin, 1981; Schachter & Stone, 1985b). As we begin our discussion of these environmental experiences, we must again focus on factors that are shared by siblings leading to sibling similarity, and those that are not shared leading to sibling differences.

ENVIRONMENTAL INFLUENCES: SHARED AND NOT SHARED BY SIBLINGS

Perhaps the most surprising finding of contemporary behavior genetics is that environmental experiences shared in common by all children in the family, such as their social class, play virtually no role in the development of personality and psychopathology, in themselves. Instead, it is the environmental factors the siblings do not share in common, such as preferential treatment of one sibling, that account for the influence of the environment on the development of psychopathology.

This finding is surprising because almost all developmental research on environmental influences on psychopathology has focused on shared environmental factors rather than on those that are not shared by siblings. The list of shared environmental factors, as shown in Table 2, includes such familiar variables as child rearing styles of the parents, divorce, and maternal employment. These variables are familiar because hundreds of studies have examined their effects. On the other hand, the list of environmental influences not shared by siblings, listed in Table 3, are less familiar. With the exception of birth order and spacing, they have been neglected in developmental research. Table 3 includes accidental traumatic factors, sibling interaction, differential treatment of children by their parents, nonfamily factors, and interactions of parent and child characteristics. In the latter case, for

Table 2

Environmental Influences Shared by Siblings

Social Class

Religion

Home Features (# books, # rooms)

Nutrition

Parental Values

Parental Modelling

Neighborhood Features

Child Rearing Styles

Family Size

Divorce

Maternal Employment

Father Presence/Absence

Note: With minor exceptions, these experiences are shared by all children in the same family.

Table 3

Environmental Influences Not Shared by Siblings

Accidental Factors

    Perinatal trauma

    Physical illness

    Separation

Sibling Interaction

    Differential treatment of one sibling by the other

    Deidentification

Family Structure

    Birth order

    Sibling spacing

Parental Treatment

    Differential treatment of children

    Interactions of parent and child characteristics

Nonfamily Networks

    Peer group members not shared by siblings

    Relatives

    Teachers

    Television

    Cultural change

Note: Table adapted from "The importance of nonshared (E_1) environmental influences in behavioral development," by David C. Rowe and Robert Plomin, 1981, Developmental Psychology, 17, p. 524. Copyright 1981 by the American Psychological Association. Adapted by permission.

example, divorce may have different effects on children in the same family (see Shapiro & Wallace, this volume).

What is the evidence that environmental factors which siblings share in common (those listed in Table 2) play almost no role in the development of psychopathology? The most striking evidence comes from adoption studies. If the common environment were important, we would expect adoptive children to resemble their adoptive parents in psychopathology, but they do not. They resemble their biological parents (DeFries & Plomin, 1978; Jary & Stewart, 1985; Rosenthal, 1971). On the other hand, evidence of the importance of environmental factors that siblings do not share in common (those listed in Table 3) comes from studies of identical twins. For example, among identical twins reared together, 45% of the twins become schizophrenic when the co-twin is schizophrenic (Rowe & Plomin, 1981), although their genes are identical, and they share a common household environment. It is unique environmental experiences that differ from twin to twin that must account for the fact that, in the remaining 55% of identical twins, one of the pair becomes schizophrenic while the other does not.

Because research has focused on environmental factors that siblings share in common, we know relatively little about these environmental factors that differ from sibling to sibling. In the section that follows, we will summarize what we do know about these factors and attempt to derive implications for the clinician and the educator.

ACCIDENTAL FACTORS

Accidental factors refer to different kinds of trauma to which an infant or young child may be exposed including perinatal problems and separations. For example, perinatal traumas include exposures to teratogenic agents (harmful chemical compounds, radiation), problems during delivery, and postnatal complications. These factors are classified as not shared by siblings because the exact teratogenic exposures, complications at delivery, or other perinatal traumas most often differ from one sibling to another. As severe traumas involve a relatively small proportion of all births, these influences probably explain only a small part of the total group of children at risk for childhood behavioral disorders; nevertheless, for a particular child, a perinatal trauma may account for the later development of problems.

It is noteworthy that many children seem able to recover from exposure to perinatal risk factors. In this regard, consider the comparison of genetically identical twins of different birth weights (Wilson, 1985). Identical twins are occasionally born with different birth weights, as though one twin were trying to monopolize prenatal nutrients at the expense of the weaker twin. At first, during infancy, the intellectual development (a barometer for the absence of brain damage) of the low birthweight twin is significantly delayed in comparison with the cotwin of normal birth weight. This twin, however, plays a game of catch-up, and by the period of middle childhood, both twins have the same intellectual abilities. Wilson's findings may mean that when the underlying genotype of the child is normal (as indicated by the normal-developing twin), a low birth weight can be overcome. In some cases, on the other hand, the effects of perinatal insults are more enduring. Sameroff and Chandler (1975), reviewing research on perinatal casualties, found that the effects of prematurity tend to be more lasting in lower-class children.

In this post-Freudian era, most clinicians and educators are alert to traumatic factors, both physical and psychological. Sibling comparison, however, offers a unique opportunity to evaluate the role of the trauma in the development of psychopathology. If the sibling exposed to the trauma develops psychopathology whereas the other sibling(s) does (do) not, then it seems plausible to speculate that the trauma may be one of the determinants of the psychopathology; hence, careful histories of the siblings should prove useful in clinical assessment.

SIBLING INTERACTION

Another source of sibling differences may be sibling interactions. Interactions between siblings can lead to differences because one sibling treats the other differently or because they adopt different roles in the family. For example, an aggressive child may provoke conflicts with other, more submissive family members. Patterson (1984) has found in families in which one child was clinic-referred for aggression that the siblings also tend to be above average in their level of aggression. "Coercive cycles" of conflict between sibling partners make for high levels of family violence. The labelled "deviant" child, however, was not exactly the same in the display of aggression as the sibling's because his/her level of aggression was higher and more often directed toward the mother. As the labelled child is "different," this raises the possibility that constitutional factors (nonshared genes) contribute to the enduring difference between the problem child and his/her siblings. On the other hand, if sibling interaction contributes to this child's aggressive behavior, clinical intervention aimed at altering sibling interaction might be effective. In Patterson's clinical interventions, the focus has certainly broadened in recent years to emphasize both parent-child and sibling interaction.

Role theory emphasizes that siblings in a family may have different perceived roles. One child may be the scapegoat and receive blame for the family's problems, or one child might excel academically while another is good at sports. In families in which the mother is working or in large families, it is not uncommon for older siblings to provide care for younger siblings. Schachter (this volume) proposes that siblings seek their identities in different behavioral styles, a process of "deidentification," because then each sibling can succeed while averting sibling rivalry. Again, it is very important to identify the way in which children acquire various roles within a family. To some extent, the selection of a role may depend on the child's characteristics (e.g., the more nurturant sibling taking the caring role). Conversely, the assignment of a role to a child might affect that child's characteristics. For the present, the clinician or educator may want to investigate how children in a family seem to acquire their particular family "role," and how that role might be used in the process of therapeutic intervention.

That siblings adopt different roles does not mean that their interactions are different in every respect. Rowe and Plomin (1981) summarized some data on sibling interaction showing that sibling affection tended to be mutual. That is, when one sibling liked the other, that emotion tended to be reciprocated. While in other cases, both siblings disliked one another. When the clinician or educator is dealing with a child who has a behavioral diagnosis, it becomes important to collect data on the "normal" sibling(s) to explore the nature of sibling interactions as perceived by family members.

FAMILY STRUCTURE

If any conclusion can be reached about the effects of sibling status variables (e.g., birth order, spacing) on personality, it is that the findings to date are inconsistent (Ernst & Angst, 1983). Intuitions about birth order effects are common, but often contradictory. Older siblings may be anxious because parents place more demands for responsibility on them, but younger siblings may be anxious because they lack the power held by older brothers and sisters. The ease with which hypotheses about family structure can be generated emphasizes the importance of actual verification of each hypothesis.

It should be noted, however, that the inconsistent findings to date are based almost entirely on comparing children from different families. For example, a group of firstborns is compared with a group of second-borns from other families or a group of third-borns from yet another set of families. Studies comparing firstborns and later-borns from the same family, and controlling for age differences at the same time, have been rare. We must await the results of such studies before we can conclude definitively that such variables as birth order and spacing produce no consistent effects on behavior. In the meantime, clinicians and educators are urged to be wary about attempts to explain personality or psychopathology on the basis of such sibling status variables as birth order and spacing.

Differential Treatment by Parents

If parents treat their children differently, for example, if they prefer one child over the others, if they label one as "bad" and the other as "good," or if they are more punitive toward one than the other(s), these disparities could account for differences between siblings in personality or psychopathology. What is the evidence that parents do, in fact, treat their children differently?

A number of studies have failed to find differences in the way parents treat their children (Cohen, Dibble & Grawe, 1977; Daniels & Plomin, 1985; Dunn, Plomin & Nettles, 1985; Owen, Adams, Forest, Stolz & Fischer, 1971; Rowe & Elam, 1986). With rare exception, however, these studies have been limited in methodology. For example, they depend on parent reports, and parents may be unwilling to admit to giving one child favored treatment, or they depend on the reports of siblings themselves and siblings may be unwilling to admit that one is favored over the other. Yet, another study (Dunn, Plomin & Nettles, 1985) is based on infant observation, but parents may treat infants similarly and treat older siblings differently. Given these methodological limitations, it may be that some important differences in the way parents treat their children have been overlooked.

A recent study of adolescents by Daniels, Dunn, Furstenberg and Plomin (1985) suggests that this may be the case. Daniels et al. (1985) found that the more delinquent sibling, relative to a brother or sister, experienced less maternal closeness and fewer parental chore expectations. Similarly, the sibling who was more emotionally distressed had received less maternal affection and less peer friendliness. This finding needs to be replicated and further research in this area is needed, but it is an important finding for the clinician and educator. It suggests that practitioners should be alert to the possibility of parents treating their children differently and should be prepared to intervene to promote the mental health of the sibling who is not treated as well as the other(s).

NONFAMILY NETWORKS

As siblings grow older, they spend less time in the common family household and more time in diverse nonfamily settings. They often acquire different friends. They take classes from different teachers and join in different extracurricular activities. In times of rapid cultural change, siblings may experience different social pressures at different stages. Given the waning power of the family relative to nonfamily influences, the latter influences may be of particular importance for the different developmental courses siblings follow.

Of the nonfamily influences mentioned in Table 3, peer group members not shared by siblings, relatives, teachers, television, and cultural change, the most important influence on psychopathology is probably the peer group. In the study by Daniels and Plomin (1985), peer group characteristics were seen by adolescents as more differentiated than those of the siblings' mutual interactions or parental treatments. Moreover, a number of theorists have suggested that peer influences are significant. Sullivan (1953) saw a close "chum" in childhood as contributing to psychological development by providing a source of self-validation outside of the family, and an accepting "chum," according to Sullivan, might compensate for strained parent-child relationships. Peers may be important because they provide an equal-status context in which children can learn role-taking and rule-making skills fundamental to social interaction and moral development (Piaget, 1932). Learning theorists regard the peer group as providing the role-models for both prosocial and antisocial behavior. For example, peers may teach aggressive behaviors to unaggressive younger children (although they may also be children with genetic tendencies towards aggression).

One of the best replicated findings in the delinquency literature is that delinquent youths tend to associate with friends who are also delinquent (West & Farrington, 1977). In addition, poor peer relations are an excellent indicator of later psychopathology (Campbell & Cluss, 1982). Moreover, most learning of sexual behaviors is attributed to peer teaching (with peers sometimes as ignorant as those they seek to inform). Given these theoretical and empirical results, peer relations appear to play an important role in the development of childhood psychopathology, especially as children become adolescents.

Like other correlations, the relationship between the quality of peer group characteristics and the characteristics of a child cannot solve the riddle of which comes first, the chicken or the egg. A child's disordered peer relationships may be a partial cause of a child's behavior problems, or they can be interpreted as symptomatic of problems within the child that lead him to select particular types of friends or to use poor methods of forging friendships. Even when poor peer relationships are noncausal, they may reinforce inadequate behavioral patterns, and worsen a situation. For these reasons, clinicians and educators need to evaluate a child's peer relationships, especially for older children. Other nonfamily environmental influences are more difficult to study. Most people can cite a former teacher whose influence on them was powerful and lasting, but what that teacher may have done with the student may not have been out of the ordinary. A professor tells of discussing the standard topics of introductory psychology with a nun, only to learn later that she perceived these student-teacher conversations as formative in the decision to leave her order. He did not mean to lead a nun astray. It is puzzling that the impact of environmental experiences that are unique to each sibling sometimes depends on a convergence of circumstances that is itself unique.

What of the Wideman brothers, John, the university professor, and Robert, the convicted murderer? How can we account for their vastly different life outcomes? John Wideman in his book *Brothers and Keepers* (1984) cites a number of different environmental experiences. Perhaps most important was the invasion of the drug culture into their urban ghetto during the vulnerable adolescent years of Robert, who is the younger brother. Altogether, John was a child of the quiet fifties, Robert of the tumultuous sixties. In fact, Robert was leader of a 1968 student revolt that succeeded in ousting the principal of his high school. Robert recalls the drug invasion during that fateful year (Wideman, 1984, p. 117):

> Sixty-eight is when the dope came in real heavy too. I mean you could always get dope but in '68 seems like they flooded [the ghetto]. Easy as buying a quart of milk. Could cop your works in a drugstore. Dope was everywhere that summer. Cats ain't never touched the stuff before got into dope and dope got into them. A bitch, man. It come like a flood. Me. I start to using heavy that summer. Just like everybody else I knew.

There were also lifelong differences in the brothers' temperaments or personalities, with Robert less likely to comply with adult discipline and adult values. John was good at school and good at sports. Robert was defined as wild, always in trouble, a rebel. Thomas and Chess (1977), based on their theory of temperament, would probably classify John as an "easy" child and Robert as a "difficult" child and attribute these temperamental differences mainly to genetic factors. On the other hand, Schachter and Stone (1985a, also see this volume) might attribute these differences to the environmental process of sibling deidentification, the tendency of siblings to define themselves (and others to define them) as different or contrasting in personality. Note how Robert defines himself by contrast to John (Wideman, 1984, p. 85):

> Me and trouble hooked up. See, it was a question of being somebody. Being my own person. Like youns had sports and good grades sewed up. Wasn't nothing I could do in school or sports that youns hadn't done already . . . Had to get out from under youns' good grades and do. Way back then I decided I wanted to be a star. I wanted to make it big, my way . . . Had to figure out a new territory. I had to be a rebel. . . .

To try to assess the relative importance of hereditary and environmental influences on the Wideman brothers would take us too far afield. The case, however, does serve to illustrate how a variety of genetic and environmental influences unique to each sibling can lead to very different outcomes. Clinicians and educators are urged to pay close attention to these formative factors unique to each sibling.

CONCLUSIONS

We have seen that when one child in the family develops the symptoms of a behavior disorder, his/her sibling(s) is(are) not likely to acquire the disorder. To understand this phenomenon, it is useful to adopt a four-fold model partitioning genetic and environmental influences into those shared by siblings and those which siblings do not share in common. For those childhood disorders where heredity appears to play a role, including the externalizing disorders and autism, shared genes may help explain why siblings might develop the same disorder. Whereas different genes might explain why one sibling becomes mentally ill and another remains unaffected.

Environment to appears to play a crucial role in the development of psychopathology, even for those disorders where genetic factors seem important. For example, estimates suggest that heredity and environment play equally important roles in the development of schizophrenia.

Finally, and perhaps most important, contemporary behavior genetics helps us understand how environmental experiences contribute to the development of psychopathology. Surprisingly, twin and adoption studies show that the common environmental factors shared by children in the same family, such as their social class or the absence of their father, do not play a significant determining role in the development of psychopathology. Instead, these studies call attention to the role of environmental experiences that are unique to each sibling in the family including accidental traumatic factors, sibling interaction, differential parental treatment, and nonfamily factors. It is these different experiences, together with different genes, that help to explain why in most cases, siblings of children with behavior disorders do not themselves develop the disorder.

REFERENCES

Campbell, S. B. & Cluss, P. (1982). Peer relationships of young children with behavior problems. In K. H. Rubin & H. S. Ross (Eds.), *Peer relationships and social skills in childhood* (pp. 323-351). New York: Springer-Verlag.

Cantwell, D. P. (1975). Genetic studies of hyperactive children: Psychiatric illness in biological and adopting parents. In R. R. Fieve, D. Rosenthal & H. Brill (Eds.), *Genetic research in psychiatry* (pp. 273-280). Baltimore: Johns Hopkins University.

Cohen, D. J., Dibble, E. & Grave, J. M. (1977). Parental style: Mothers' and fathers' perceptions of their relations with twin children. *Archives of General Psychiatry, 34*, 445-451.

Daniels, D., Dunn, J., Furstenberg, F. F., Jr. & Plomin, R. (1985). Environmental differences within the family and adjustment differences within pairs of adolescent siblings. *Child Development. 56*, 764-774.

Daniels, D. & Plomin, R. (1985). Differential experience of siblings in the same family. *Developmental Psychology, 21*, 747-760.

DeFries, J. C. & Plomin, R. (1978). Behavioral genetics. In M. R. Rosenzweig & L. W. Porter (Eds.), *Annual review of psychology* (Vol. 29, pp. 473-515). Palo Alto, CA: Annual Reviews.

Dunn, J. F., Plomin, R. & Nettles, M. (1985). Consistency of mothers' behavior toward infant siblings. *Developmental Psychology, 21*, 1188-1195.

Ernst, C. & Angst, J. (1983). *Birth order: Its influence on personality.* Berlin: Springer-Verlag.

Graham, P. & Stevensen, J. (1985). A twin study of genetic influences on behavioral deviance. *Journal of the American Academy of Child Psychiatry, 24,* 33-41.

Jary, M. L. & Stewart, M. A. (1985). Psychiatric disorder in the parents of adopted children with aggressive conduct disorder. *Neuropsychobiology, 13,* 7-11.

Morrison, J. R. & Stewart, M. A. (1973). The psychiatric status of the legal families of adopted hyperactive children. *Archives of General Psychiatry, 28,* 1888-1891.

Owen, F. W., Adams, P. A., Forrest, T., Stolz, L. M. & Fisher, S. (1971). Learning disorders in children: Sibling studies. *Monographs of the Society for Research in Child Development, 36,*(4, Serial No. 144).

Patterson, G. R. (1984). Siblings: Fellow travelers in coercive family processes. In R. J. Blanchard & D. C. Blanchard (Eds.), *Advances in the study of aggression* (pp. 173-215). Orlando: Academic Press.

Piaget, J. (1965). *The moral judgment of the child.* New York: Free Press.

Ritvo, E. R., Freeman, B. J., Mason-Brothers, A., Mo, A. & Ritvo, A. M. (1985). Concordance for the syndrome of autism in 40 pairs of afflicted twins. *American Journal of Psychiatry, 142,* 74-77.

Rosenthal, D. (1971). *Genetics of psychopathology.* New York: McGraw-Hill Company.

Rowe, D. C. & Elam, P. (1986). *Sibling interaction styles and child rearing styles: A study of siblings and their parents.* Manuscript submitted for publication.

Rowe, D. C. & Osgood, D. W. (1984). Heredity and sociological theories of delinquency: A reconsideration. *American Sociological Review, 49,* 526-540.

Rowe, D. C. & Plomin, R. (1981). The importance of nonshared (E₁) environmental influences in behavioral development. *Developmental Psychology, 17,* 517-531.

Safer, D. J. (1973). A familial factor in minimal brain dysfunction. *Behavior Genetics, 3,* 175-186.

Sameroff, A. J. & Chandler, M. J. (1975). Reproductive risk and the continuum of caretaking casualty. In F. D. Horowitz, E. M. Hetherington, S. Scarr-Salapatek & G. M. Siegel (Eds.), *Review of child development research* (Vol. 4). Chicago: University of Chicago Press.

Schachter, F. F. & Stone, R. K. (1985a). Difficult sibling, easy sibling: Temperament and the within-family environment. *Child Development, 56,* 1335-1344.

Schachter, F. F. & Stone, R. K. (1985b). Pediatricians' and psychologists' implicit personality theory: Significance of sibling differences. *Journal of Developmental and Behavioral Pediatrics, 6,* 295-297.

Sullivan, H. S. (1953). *The interpersonal theory of psychiatry.* New York: Norton.

Thomas, A. & Chess, S. (1977). *Temperament and development.* New York: Bruner/Mazel.

Twito, T. J. & Stewart, M. A. (1982). A half-sibling study of aggressive conduct disorder. *Neuropsychobiology, 8,* 144-150.

Welner, Z., Welner, A., Stewart, M., Palkes, H. & Wish, E. (1977). A controlled study of siblings of hyperactive children. *Journal of Nervous and Mental Disease, 165,* 110-117.

West, D. J. & Farrington, D. P. (1977). *The delinquent way of life.* London: William Heinemann Ltd.

Wideman, J. E. (1984). *Brothers and keepers.* New York: Holt, Rinehart & Winston.

Wilson, R. S. (1985). Risk and resilience in early mental development. *Developmental Psychology, 21,* 795-805.

Sibling Relationships
and Adjustment of Children
with Disabled Brothers and Sisters

Susan M. McHale, PhD
Wendy C. Gamble, PhD

SUMMARY. Research on children with disabled siblings reveals that these youngsters may treat their siblings more kindly and spend more time caring for them than do children with nondisabled siblings. Their experiences may produce more worries and anxieties; however, these children also may develop more tolerance and humanitarian concerns. Characteristics of disabled siblings and the children themselves as well as family circumstance may affect children's reactions. Interventions for promoting positive sibling relations and personal adjustment include behavioral training in managing and coping with the disabled child, sibling support groups, and parent education programs designed to foster understanding of the special needs of these youngsters.

Sometimes he likes me to show him books. He looks at the pictures and I tell him the stories. One time he took my library book and ripped some of the pages. I got mad at him, but I know it's not really his fault. He doesn't really understand.

Jenny, Age 9

Susan M. McHale is Associate Professor of Human Development, College of Human Development, The Pennsylvania State University, University Park, PA 16802.

Wendy C. Gamble is Post-doctoral Fellow, Department of Psychology, University of Denver, University Park, CO 80208.

The authors would like to thank Vicki Harris and Terese Hritcko for their help in conducting this research and Joy Barger for her help in preparing this paper. They also are very grateful to the families who participated in their research. Funding for this research was provided by the March of Dimes Foundation.

As these remarks by a child with a mentally retarded brother suggest, growing up with a sibling who has a handicapping condition has both its bright and bleak moments. The two sides of these sibling relationships seem to be evident to children even at a young age. As with most siblings, a warm and harmonious relationship can also be a source of distress, anger, and jealousy.

From other parts in this volume, we have seen that sibling relationships are unique in several important respects, and these special properties of sibling relationships may exert a significant influence on children's socialization. Brothers and sisters usually spend large amounts of time together, over many years, and, in doing so, come to share experiences that they will share with no one else (Bank & Kahn, 1982). Siblings often serve as playmates for one another, but children also learn new roles, such as those of teacher, caregiver, or "leader" for a younger (or less capable) brother or sister (Cicirelli, 1976; Dunn, 1983; Samuels, 1980). Research focused specifically on children with disabled siblings indicates that these children's relationships share many of the same characteristics. Yet, there are some important differences as well. Just as experiences with nondisabled siblings seem to exert an important influence on children's social, emotional, and mental development, the special experiences children have with disabled siblings may have unique consequences for their well-being and development.

Our first goal is to describe the nature of children's relationships with disabled siblings. Second, we examine the links between children's sibling relationships and their personal adjustment. Third, we review other factors contributing to the adjustment of children with disabled siblings.

The reader should keep in mind the difficulties of drawing general conclusions from the existing research. There is tremendous diversity in the way families cope with a disabled child and extensive differences among disabled children themselves. In addition, research findings using diverse methods and samples sometimes are inconsistent. Further, and probably most important, the availability of community programs as well as public awareness of the needs and rights of disabled individuals have been changing over the past decade. Such changes mean that many families will experience a more supportive context for rearing a disabled child than did families in the past (McHale, Simeonsson & Sloan, 1984). Consequently, yesterday's research may not always apply to tomorrow's families with disabled children. In view of these changes, we have tried, whenever possible, to focus on recent research including our own data collected in the last few years.

CHARACTERISTICS OF SIBLING RELATIONSHIPS

Feelings About the Sibling Relationship

We have noted that most sibling relationships involve both rivalry and conflict on the one hand and support and affection on the other. For the most part, however, parents of disabled children describe the relationship between their disabled and nondisabled children as basically positive with any difficulties being temporary and remediable (Holt, 1958; Lloyd-Bostock, 1976). Based on parent reports, one study indicates that only about 13% of the children have disturbed relationships with their handicapped siblings, and that most parents believe the problems between their children are not greater than would be seen in pairs of nondisabled brothers and sisters (Lonsdale, 1978).

Children also report positive feelings about their handicapped siblings. When young adolescents were asked about their relationships with a handicapped brother or sister, for example, they demonstrated a general acceptance and tolerance toward the child (Gralicker, Fishler & Koch, 1962) and reported that the child had brought pleasure to their own and their families' lives (Caldwell & Guze, 1960). Adults who looked back on their family life and on growing up with a handicapped sibling also said that they had had generally good relationships with that child (Cleveland & Miller, 1977).

In our own research, we have asked youngsters between the ages of 8 and 14 who had younger mentally retarded siblings to rate "how happy" they were with seven dimensions of their sibling relationships (see Table 1). Our analyses revealed that the youngsters, on the average, were moderately happy with all dimensions. We proceeded to compare the ratings of boys and girls with and without mentally retarded siblings and found that they differed only on one dimension, how children "get along" with their siblings. As Table 1 shows, children with disabled siblings rated themselves as being more satisfied in this domain.

Children's Positive and Negative Behaviors Toward Siblings

The results of research on children's feelings about their sibling relationships are consistent with the findings of other studies in which mothers, fathers, and children have been interviewed and asked to rate children's behavior (such as the extent of fighting and arguing or help and support) toward their disabled siblings.

Table 1

Ratings of Satisfaction with Domains of the Sibling Relationship

by Children with Younger Nondisabled and Disabled Siblings

(N=62)

Relationship Domains	Children with Younger:				
	Nondisabled Siblings		Disabled Siblings		
	Boys	Girls	Boys	Girls	Statistical Tests
(1) Time Spent with Sibling	6.5	6.9	6.6	5.9	
(2) Time Spent in Caregiving	6.1	6.5	6.5	7.4	
(3) How Sibs Get Along	6.0	5.6	7.2	7.2	G
(4) How Much Child is Boss	7.1	5.9	6.3	6.5	
(5) Parents' Treatment of Child vs. Sib	6.4	5.3	6.5	5.4	s
(6) Parents' Attention to Child vs. Sib	6.7	5.8	6.9	6.9	
(7) Overall Satisfaction with Relationship	7.6	7.9	8.1	8.6	

Note: Ratings range from 1 (very unhappy) to 9 (very happy).

G = Difference between children with disabled and nondisabled siblings is

significant (p < .01).

s = Sex difference approaches significance (p < .10).

Although some ratings showed no differences in behavior between children with disabled and nondisabled siblings, whenever sibling differences were found, however, they favored those with disabled siblings (McHale & Gamble, 1984; McHale, Simeonsson & Sloan, 1984; Ogle, 1982; Shaeffer & Edgerton, 1981). For example, children with disabled siblings as compared to those with nondisabled siblings were rated by parents as behaving more kindly and less aggressively toward their siblings. Children also rated themselves as behaving less aggressively toward their disabled siblings.

These findings on behavior ratings need to be supplemented by more objective measures. In our own research, we have taken a first step in this direction by collecting behavior reports from our sample of 8- to 14-year-olds. We used a diary-like procedure. We telephoned the children on a daily basis to obtain detailed reports of their behavior during their interactions and activities with their siblings. Specifically, we called them on seven evenings, shortly before their bedtimes, and we asked them to report on their sibling interactions and activities during the day of the call. We used this kind of procedure rather than observing sibling behavior in the home because we reasoned that, for children this age, both fighting (negative behaviors) and supportive interactions (positive behaviors) might occur only a few times a day. This would make it difficult to obtain an accurate picture of how siblings get along if they were observed even for several hours. Moreover, youngsters at this age may be disinclined to fight with their siblings, especially a disabled sibling, when someone is watching.

Using behavior reports from the telephone interviews, we found no differences between children with younger disabled and nondisabled siblings in the number of negative or positive behaviors that they directed toward these siblings. On the other hand, girls more often than boys reported that their younger siblings behaved in negative ways toward them whether the sibling was disabled or not. Being an older sister of a disabled child has been shown to be associated with a greater risk for adjustment problems, and several investigators have suggested that this increased vulnerability may be due to the fact that older sisters are required to spend more time in caregiving activities with their siblings

(Cleveland & Miller, 1977; Farber, 1959; Grossman, 1972). Our data suggest that the problem may not be caregiving time per se, but how disabled children behave when they are being cared for by their siblings that may be the problem for these girls. If this is true, it may not be as important to change the way family responsibilities are assigned as it is to teach children behavior management strategies that they can use when interacting with their siblings. As we will see, such training programs have been implemented with some positive consequences. This issue of which children with disabled siblings are at greater risk for adjustment problems is one that will arise repeatedly in our discussion.

The Nature and Intensity of Sibling Problems

We have been discussing whether children with disabled brothers and sisters have feelings and behaviors that are more positive or more negative than those of children with nondisabled siblings. Alternatively, we might ask whether the kinds of problems siblings experience in these two situations are neither better nor worse but simply different. Our own data indicate that this is indeed the case. We asked children to describe, in an open-ended way, the kind and the intensity of problems that they experienced on a daily basis with their younger disabled and nondisabled siblings (Gamble, 1985). This information was collected in five of the nightly telephone interviews we described earlier. Altogether, 58 youngsters (half with disabled and half with nondisabled siblings) described 190 problem events (an average of 3.25 events per child in a five-day period). These problem events were classified into nine categories shown in Table 2.

Table 2 shows that there were no differences, overall, in the *total* number of problems reported by children with disabled versus nondisabled siblings. Children with disabled siblings, however, reported experiencing Problem 2, the younger sibling is hurt or sick, and Problem 7, the older sibling is concerned about the younger sibling's emotional well-being, relatively more often than did children with nondisabled siblings. As we might expect, concern for a sibling's emotional and physical well-being is more of an issue when that sibling has special needs. Children with nondisabled siblings, on the other hand, reported experiencing

Table 2

Sibling Problems Reported by Children with

Younger Nondisabled and Disabled Siblings

(N=58)

		Children with Younger:		
		Nondisabled Siblings	Disabled Siblings	Statistical Tests
I.	Average Number of Problem Events	3.34	3.17	
II.	Proportions of Specific Kinds of Problems			
	Problem 1: Sib's behavior is different or "weird"	.094	.063	
	Problem 2: Sib is hurt or sick	.073	.170	G
	Problem 3: Child does something negative to Sib	.010	.032	
	Problem 4: Sib does something negative to Child	.333	.320	
	Problem 5: Child and Sib are mutually negative	.083	.020	G
	Problem 6: Sib is naughty	.188	.170	
	Problem 7: Child is concerned about Sib's emotional well-being	.010	.064	G
	Problem 8: Child can't do something because of Sib	.115	.074	
	Problem 9: Sib gets upset even though Child hasn't behaved negatively	.094	.085	

G = Differences between children with nondisabled and disabled siblings are significant ($p < .05$).

Problem 5, mutual fights, relatively more often than did the children with disabled siblings. Mutual fights are less likely to occur or less likely to be acknowledged by children with disabled siblings probably because disabled children are less capable of reciprocating and also because the nondisabled sibling may feel guilty and uncomfortable about such unequal battles.

In addition to asking children what kinds of problems they had with their siblings, we also asked them to evaluate the "intensity" of their problems. The results of group comparisons suggested that sibling difficulties were seen as "bigger" problems by children with disabled brothers and sisters. That is, even though the number of sibling problem events was similar in both groups, these events were seen as more troublesome by children with disabled siblings.

Coping with Sibling Problems

Recent research suggests that it may not be stress itself, but how effectively we cope with it that determines our mental health. Some investigators have gone so far as to suggest that children who are not confronted with challenges as they grow up may have more adjustment problems as adults because they have never learned effective coping strategies (Kagan, 1983). Thus, it seemed important to examine the way children cope with the problems presented by their disabled siblings. As such coping strategies have not been studied before, we began by developing our own classification scheme based on the children's reports in our nightly phone conversations. We divided their behaviors into four categories. Children could react to sibling problems by *doing* something actively, such as by (a) hitting or yelling at their sibling or (b) going outside to play and forget about their problem. They could also react by *thinking* about the situation and (c) telling themselves to ignore the sibling or (d) thinking mean thoughts about the sibling. Another way of describing these responses is that children could direct their coping efforts *toward themselves* (examples b and c above) or *toward others* (examples a and d).

Analyses of the children's coping behaviors revealed both differences and similarities in the ways children with disabled and nondisabled siblings reacted. Responses involving direct actions, either positive actions (helping) or negative actions (hitting), were reported more frequently by children with disabled siblings, particularly when the younger sibling's behaviors were likely to affect the other sibling directly (such as when the younger sibling's behaviors were deliberate and aversive). When the younger sibling was sick or uncontrolled, children were more likely to react by having thoughts or ideas about another person (e.g., "I hope he's not going to have to go to the hospital again," "Why can't Mom make him stop?," or "He can't help it"). It may be that when a sibling is hurt or sick, the older child can do little to remedy the situation, so that thoughts replace actions. Finally, it is interesting that avoidant responses (such as doing something fun to try to forget the problem) were rare for both groups of children, even though these kinds of coping strategies were associated with lower levels of anxiety, as we note later in this paper in the section on adjustment.

Children's Activities and Roles with Their Siblings

In addition to the way brothers and sisters treat each other, other important dimensions of sibling relationships pertain to how much time children spend together and to the kinds of activities they undertake. The results of some studies suggest that children's activities with disabled siblings tend to be more instrumental (helping, teaching, and caregiving) in contrast to those of nondisabled siblings which are more often expressive in nature, as in play (McHale & Gamble, 1987; Miller, 1974; Stoneman & Brody, 1984). In our own work, we have attempted to develop a detailed picture of children's daily activities with their disabled and nondisabled siblings by using the telephone diary procedure. As Table 3 shows, children with disabled siblings spend significantly more time taking care of their siblings whereas children with nondisabled siblings spend more time doing chores together. (Table 3 also shows a trend for girls, as a group, to spend more time in caregiving than do boys.) Some researchers have suggested that the extra caregiving activities of children with disabled siblings may be a source of adjustment problems in these youngsters. Later in this paper we will examine this issue.

In this same study, mothers also were interviewed by telephone during the evening (on seven occasions) and asked to report on the frequency and duration of children's household chores each day (including making beds, preparing meals, caring for pets, and straightening up the house). We reasoned that it may not be sibling caregiver per se which would be the source of adjustment problems when children have disabled siblings. In-

Table 3

Durations of Siblings' Activities and Household Tasks of Children
with Younger Nondisabled and Disabled Siblings
(N=62)

	Children with Younger:				
	Nondisabled Siblings		Disabled Siblings		Statistical Tests
	Boys	Girls	Boys	Girls	
I. Durations of Daily Activities with Siblings (in minutes)					
Take Care of Siblings	8.5	16.1	17.9	25.3	G
Do Chores with Sibling	7.8	17.4	2.5	3.1	G s
Eat Meals Together	35.1	31.0	35.5	37.4	
Watch TV Together	40.3	35.7	43.3	25.7	
Go on Outings Together	43.8	47.6	38.0	60.6	
Play Together	24.1	12.8	21.8	15.9	
Total Duration of Activities with Sibling	160.0	157.6	159.0	167.9	
II. Duration of Daily Household Tasks (in minutes)	44.2	73.4	58.9	91.8	S g

G = Difference between children with disabled and nondisabled siblings is
significant ($p < .05$).

g = Difference between children with disabled and nondisabled siblings
approaches significance ($p < .10$).

S = Sex difference is significant ($p < .05$).

s = Sex difference approaches significance ($p < .10$).

stead, these children may be responsible for more household duties because of the extra time their parents must spend caring for
the disabled child. Comparisons of the household tasks of boys
and girls with disabled and nondisabled siblings also are shown
in Table 3. Consistent with previous literature, our data revealed
that there is a tendency for children with disabled siblings to

spend more time on household tasks. More striking than the group differences, however, were the differences between boys and girls in the time spent on chores, with girls spending almost twice as much time.

SUMMARY AND CONCLUSIONS

Before leaving our discussion of the relationships of disabled and nondisabled siblings and how they compare to those of other children, it may be useful to summarize what we know. Our reading of the data leads us to conclude that, for school-age children and young adolescents, these relationships tend to be more positive than negative in their feeling tone. Furthermore, children with disabled siblings appear to have more positive and fewer negative behavioral interactions than do those with nondisabled siblings on some measures (behavior ratings), though not on others (behavior reports).

A look at children's descriptions of their problems suggests the following: First, even though the number of problems reported may be the same or less for children with disabled siblings as compared to those with nondisabled siblings, children with disabled siblings see those problems as more troublesome. Second, children with disabled siblings seem to have problems that are less obvious to observers. These are "internalized problems" involving children's worries and anxieties about their disabled siblings' welfare. Although problems may not be evident to the observer, they may involve extensive emotional reactions. As we will see later in this paper, opening channels of communication with parents and with other youngsters in similar circumstances seems to be an important means of alleviating some of these worries and anxieties.

Our data on siblings' joint activities suggest that children with disabled and nondisabled siblings spend about the same amount of time together, but there are some differences in the kinds of activities the children undertake together. Specifically, children with disabled siblings spend more time in caregiving activities. In contrast, children with nondisabled siblings spend more time performing household tasks together. These differences suggest a greater degree of inequality or complementarity in the relationships of children with disabled siblings, with older siblings taking the role of leader and caregiver. Relationships between nondisabled siblings, by contrast, are more likely to be equal and reciprocal. In the following section, we will see that the different experiences of children with disabled and nondisabled siblings may have important consequences for their adjustment.

SIBLING RELATIONSHIPS AND ADJUSTMENT OF CHILDREN WITH DISABLED SIBLINGS

Are certain kinds of experiences with siblings associated with better adjustment in children? In the following pages, we review the available data on the associations between children's psychological well-being and (a) how happy children are with their sibling relationships, (b) how well they get along with their siblings, (c) how they cope with sibling problems, and (d) the extent to which they engage in particular kinds of activities with their siblings. The information to be reviewed comes primarily from our own research as there are few previous systematic investigations of these issues. We measured four indices of adjustment: depression, anxiety, self-esteem, and conduct problems.

First, we examined whether any of these four indices of well-being were correlated with children's satisfaction with their sibling relationships. In particular, we studied each of the domains listed in Table 1. The results showed that children's satisfaction with their sibling relationship, in itself, was not associated with measures of their well-being. On the other hand, children were more depressed, more anxious, and had lower self-esteem when they were dissatisfied about how their parents treated them relative to their younger siblings and/or dissatisfied with how much attention their parents gave them relative to their siblings. That is, the only domains in Table 1 that *are* significantly correlated with children's well-being pertained to children's views about how "fairly" their parents behaved toward them compared to how siblings were treated. This finding held for children with disabled siblings and those with nondisabled brothers and sisters.

We also examined the relationships between children's well-being and the extent of positive behaviors (e.g., help) and negative behaviors (e.g., fights) between the siblings. First, using mother and child behavior ratings, we found no relationship between rated behaviors and children's adjustment. Next, we looked at the correlations between children's psychological well-being and their daily behavior reports (in the telephone interviews). These analyses revealed that siblings were more likely to be depressed and anxious and have low self-esteem when their sibling relationships were characterized by negative behavior.

Next, we studied whether children's use of particular coping strategies (described above) was related to their adjustment. Our analyses revealed that the frequency with which children used "other-directed" *mental* coping strategies (such as blaming their sibling for problems or trying to understand the sibling's point of view) was positively related to their self-esteem. Moreover, children who used more self-directed *active* coping strategies (such as doing something enjoyable in order to forget about a problem) had fewer anxiety symptoms. We believe that this area represents a promising line of inquiry, and one that will have important implications for professionals who work with these youngsters. Thus far, behaviorally-based training programs for siblings have focused on teaching children behavior management strategies to use with their siblings (Powell & Ogle, 1985). These findings, as well as other findings on children's attributions about the causes of sibling conflicts (Gamble, McHale & Ballard, 1985), suggest that *children's interpretations* of their siblings' behavior and problems may be as important as observable behavior in understanding when and why children display adjustment problems. Cognitive behavioral strategies (see Meichenbaum, 1977) aimed at teaching children to "talk to themselves" in different ways about why problems occur and how to solve them, may constitute an effective set of intervention procedures that has yet to be studied in this group of children.

As we noted earlier, the extra "burdens" children are thought to assume when their siblings are disabled also are thought to be a cause of these children's adjustment problems (Cleveland & Miller, 1977; Farber, 1959; Gath, 1974; Grossman, 1972). Until recently, however, such conclusions have been speculative and based on circumstantial evidence. For instance, elder sisters tend to have more family responsibilities, and they are also the ones that are likely to have more adjustment problems. We explored this issue empirically by examining the relationships between children's involvement in caregiving and in other sibling activities and the four indices of children's well-being. The results showed only one significant correlation, between anxiety and the amount of time youngsters spend in caregiving activities, and even this correlation with anxiety was low ($r = .25, p < .05$). We also found that the extent of children's household responsibilities other than caregiving was *not* correlated with any of our measures of psychological adjustment.

Our telephone diary procedure provides information about what siblings are doing with one another, but it does not give us a picture of the more qualitative features of the siblings' joint activities. Some studies have shown that there may be advantages to disabled children when they interact with their nondisabled siblings. In such a context, their behavior is more social and more appropriate than it is when they are playing by themselves or with other disabled children (Mash & Mercer, 1979; Peltz, 1977). On the other hand, disabled children still display some degree of inappropriate play even with their siblings. For nondisabled youngsters, especially when their siblings are extremely impaired, such play experiences may not be the pleasurable, egalitarian interactions of normal peer play. Instead, these nondisabled youngsters may attempt to entertain siblings, keep them out of mischief, or teach them new skills. In this respect, these youngsters may not experience the same degree of emotional support, sharing of perspectives, and give and take that they would if their siblings were more similar in mental, emotional, and social development. Children also may feel resentment at continually having to assume the role of "leader" and "organizer" in sibling activities. Later we describe Farber's and Ryckman's (1965) concept of "role tension" that can be applied to situations in which children who are chronologically younger take on the role of the "oldest" with a disabled sibling. Breslau (1982) argues that these younger siblings are particularly vulnerable as they resent this reversal of roles.

On the other hand, the role of teacher and caregiver may bring gratifications and learning opportunities. The benefits of growing up with a disabled sibling have been investigated in several studies. Children who have the greatest responsibility for their handicapped siblings, often display more idealism and humanitarian concern in their life goals. For example, Farber and Jenne (1963) found that teenagers who interacted frequently with their retarded brother or sister ranked making a contribution to mankind and devoting their lives to worthwhile causes as their preferred life goals. Teenagers who interacted less with their handicapped sibling, on the other hand, ranked having many friends, focusing life on marriage and family, and being respected in the community as preferred life goals.

Farber and Jenne (1963) interpreted these findings as indicating an internalization of social-welfare norms by youngsters who are more involved with their handicapped sibling. Additionally, the extent to which having a handicapped sibling affects the career choices of adults was examined by Cleveland and Miller (1977). These investigators found that oldest females in the family (the group reported to have the heaviest caretaking responsibilities for the handicapped sibling) were the ones most likely to pursue the helping professions, perhaps putting into practice such social-welfare concerns. There also is evidence that many children with handicapped siblings are characterized by greater maturity and are more responsible than their age-mates (Schreiber & Feeley, 1965). Caldwell and Guze (1960) interviewed young adolescents with mentally retarded siblings and found that these youngsters showed an increased understanding of retarded persons and, in general, were more empathic towards persons with problems. Finally, almost half of a group of college-age students interviewed by Grossman (1972) were judged to have benefited from having a handicapped sibling; they were found to be more altruistic and idealistic, more tolerant toward others, and more oriented toward humanistic concerns. These findings are in accord with anecdotes from a number of other investigators (Holt, 1958; Lloyd-Bostock, 1976; O'Neill, 1965).

These results, together with our findings of increased worries and concerns among children with disabled siblings, suggest the following picture: youngsters with disabled siblings clearly grow up in family environments that present unique challenges. In most cases, however, the stresses and problems children encounter seem surmountable. Long-term consequences are generally by no means negative; rather, taking on family responsibilities seems to foster greater maturity and keener awareness of the needs of others. Elder (1974) reached similar conclusions in a study of youngsters who grew up in another challenging context, the 1930s depression.

Not all youngsters, however, react in the same way to the challenges of life with a disabled sibling. In the following pages, we consider some of the circumstances that seem to make youngsters more or less vulnerable to adjustment problems. These conditions include: characteristics of the disabled siblings, characteristics of nondisabled siblings, and characteristics of the family and of relationships with other family members. In discussing the family, we will suggest a variety of strategies that may help children cope with the problems of growing up with a disabled sibling. For additional information about this topic, the reader is directed to a book by Powell and Ogle (1985), *Brothers and sisters: A special part of exceptional families.*

ADJUSTMENT OF CHILDREN WITH DISABLED SIBLINGS: CHILD AND FAMILY CHARACTERISTICS

The Disabled Child's Characteristics

As any one who has worked with disabled children knows, these youngsters can be very different from one another, even when they have the same diagnosis. Partly for this reason, no two children growing up with handicapped siblings will have the same experiences. Researchers have wondered why these variations occur, and they have examined the impact of such factors as the disabled child's age, diagnosis, and the severity of the disability. For instance, some investigators have suggested that, with age, a disabled child may become more difficult to manage and care for; moreover, differences between the child and his or her siblings may become more noticeable (Bristol, 1979; Farber, 1959; Wikler, 1981). In our own research we found that youngsters display more problems in adjustment when their disabled siblings are older, and these results are consistent with those of other investigators (e.g., Farber, 1964).

Results concerning the children's diagnoses have been less

consistent. Some investigators have found that the stresses experienced by family members are related to the nature of the child's disability (Holroyd & McArthur, 1976; Lavigne & Ryan, 1979: Tew & Laurence, 1973). Other investigators, however, have not found different effects (Breslau, 1982; Gath, 1972; McHale, Sloan & Simeonsson, 1986). One possibility is that the kind of disability may be less important than its severity. Farber (1959) has concluded that siblings are more adversely affected when the disabled child is more dependent and requires more care. Others have shown that mothers are similarly affected (Beckman-Bell, 1981). It has been suggested that whether or not the child is ambulatory is especially important (Tew & Laurence, 1973). Other investigators, however, have found no differences in siblings' and parents' well-being as a function of severity of the disability (Breslau, 1982; Kolin, Scherzer, New & Garfield, 1971). Indeed, one set of studies suggests that children may react more poorly to mildly disabled siblings than to severely disabled ones (Grossman, 1972; Tew & Laurence, 1973). In such cases, the disabled child's behavior may violate social expectations with little or no apparent basis for those violations. Additionally, the child may be seen as getting extra time and attention from parents for no apparent reasons. When the disability is minimal, other youngsters may conclude that a child is "bad," "stupid," or "spoiled" rather than disabled.

Siblings and parents also react to the whole child, not just his or her disability. A loud, hyperactive, uncontrollable child may be a lot more difficult to manage than a more severely disabled bedridden child who is easy to please. Such "temperament" characteristics may, in fact, be more important than the nature or severity of a child's disability (Kolin, Scherzer, New & Garfield, 1971).

The Nondisabled Child's Characteristics

The characteristics of nondisabled children also seem to make a difference in how vulnerable these youngsters are to problems. As we noted earlier, elder sisters are especially vulnerable to adjustment problems (Cleveland & Miller, 1977; Gath, 1974; Grossman, 1972; Farber, 1959). Our own data indicate that older sisters of mentally retarded children showed somewhat poorer adjustment than siblings of nondisabled children on almost every dimension we assessed (see Table 4). Older brothers of disabled children also differed from youngsters with nondisabled siblings in that they were more anxious and had lower levels of perceived competence in the areas of social acceptance and conduct. As noted earlier, adjustment problems in these children (with the exception of anxiety) were not linked to time spent in sibling caregiving or in household tasks. In addition, as we suggested earlier, emotional distress may be a likely reaction to the challenges a disabled sibling presents, though the long-term effects may not be so negative.

A reorganization of family roles can present a special challenge for children who are younger than their disabled siblings. Specifically, a child may experience "role tension" when "regardless of his birth order in the family, the severely handicapped child essentially becomes the youngest child socially," and other siblings are expected to care for him and subordinate their needs to him (Farber & Ryckman, 1965, p. 4). In explaining the special vulnerability of siblings younger than the disabled child, Breslau (1982) also argues that these youngsters never will have the chance to live in a "normal" family environment (i.e., a family not "marked" somehow by the presence of the disabled sibling). In contrast, the early years of siblings older than the disabled child may provide a buffer against later stressful circumstances.

Another process that may adversely affect siblings of disabled children is the tendency to identify with or take on the characteristics of the disabled child so that they see themselves as somehow defective (Breslau, 1982; Cleveland & Miller, 1977; Grossman, 1972; Kaplan, 1969; San Martino & Newman, 1974; Tew & Laurence, 1973). This process can affect the well-being of siblings both older *and* younger than the disabled child. Identification may be more likely when siblings are close in age, when they share similar characteristics, or when they are treated alike. Identification also may be particularly important in adolescence when youngsters are working to establish a sense of personal identity. On the basis of information obtained in discussion groups of adolescents with mentally retarded siblings, Grossman (1972) defines this problem as one in which teenagers overidentify with their retarded brother or sister. She goes on to stress the

Table 4

Measures of Psychological Well-Being of Children with

Younger Nondisabled and Disabled Siblings

CONDUCT PROBLEMS SCALE
(Goyette, Connors, & Ulrich, 1978)

Children with disabled and with nondisabled siblings show an equivalent number of conduct problems.

Boys and girls show a similar number of conduct problems.

CHILDHOOD DEPRESSION INVENTORY
(Kovacs, 1981)

Children with disabled siblings report more depression symptoms than do children with nondisabled siblings.

There is a trend for girls to report more depression symptoms than boys.

CHILDREN'S MANIFEST ANXIETY SCALE
(Reynolds & Richmond, 1979)

Children with disabled siblings report more symptoms of anxiety than do those with nondisabled siblings.

Girls and boys report a similar number of anxiety symptoms.

PERCEIVED COMPETENCE SCALE
(Harter, 1982)

General Self-Worth

Girls with disabled siblings report lower levels of general self-worth than do boys with disabled siblings or children with nondisabled siblings.

Social Acceptance

Children with disabled siblings perceive themselves as being less socially accepted than those with nondisabled siblings.

Girls and boys are similar in perceived social acceptance.

Cognitive Competence

Children with disabled and nondisabled siblings perceive themselves as equally competent in the domain of cognitive abilities.

Boys and girls perceive themselves as similar in the domain of cognitive abilities.

Perceived Conduct

Children with nondisabled siblings perceive themselves as better behaved than do those with disabled siblings.

There is a trend for girls to perceive themselves as better behaved than do boys.

importance of making children understand that they can be "normal" even though they have a retarded sibling.

In addition, professionals and parents need to communicate openly with youngsters about the nature, causes, and prognosis of their disabled sibling's condition (Grossman, 1972). Parents may believe they are protecting a child from distressing information; however, when left uninformed, children's own ideas may be even more upsetting. Due to their egocentric perspectives and "magical" thinking style, for instance, preschoolers and young school-age children may blame their sibling or even themselves for the disabling condition. That is, they may see the disability as punishment for "naughty" behavior. They also may hold the belief that somehow, through their own actions, they may magically cure their sibling. In contrast, adolescents may be especially sensitive about others' reactions to their disabled sibling because of how it reflects on their own image (cf. Elkind, 1967).

It seems safe to assume that different issues arise in the context of sibling relationships at different points in development. In our own work, we have found that youngsters' ratings of their sibling relationships become more negative with age. Moreover, age also is correlated with adjustment problems (depression, anxiety, low self-esteem) in these youngsters. Such "internalized" or emotional problems are more common in adolescents, in general, but it may be that these problems are exacerbated with youngsters who have disabled siblings.

The Family Context

Several lines of evidence point to family characteristics and parent-child relationships as important determinants of a child's reaction to a disabled sibling. For instance, children from different social class and religious backgrounds may have different experiences growing up with disabled sisters and brothers. Farber (1960), for instance, distinguishes between the "organizational crisis" of families from lower socioeconomic backgrounds (who must generate sufficient resources to meet a disabled child's needs) and the "tragic crisis" of families from middle socioeconomic status (who must resolve violated expectations regarding the disabled child's life and achievement). These different crises mean that the challenge for some youngsters will be in helping to provide care for their disabled siblings while still meeting their own needs. For others, the challenge will be to achieve a degree of acceptance of their disabled siblings' condition and life circumstances.

Families from different religious backgrounds also may have different kinds and amounts of resources available to them in coping with stresses involved in life with disabled children (Far-ber, 1959; Zuk, Miller, Bertram & Kling, 1961). In our study, mothers who were more often involved in religious activities re-ported that their families had and used more coping strategies for dealing with the stressors involved with disabled children's care. Mothers' religious involvement also was related to higher self-esteem and fewer depression and anxiety symptoms in children.

Family size also may make a difference in siblings' adjust-ment. Provided family resources are sufficient, a larger family means that the care of a disabled child can be shared by more family members (Lauterbach, 1974; Taylor, 1974). Moreover, youngsters will have several other siblings to act as models for identity formation. Finally, other nondisabled siblings can serve as a basis for social comparisons, possibly giving children evi-dence that, even if parents are spending more time and attention with the disabled sibling, they are still receiving the same kinds of parental treatment as their other nondisabled siblings.

Parent-Child Relationships

Parent-child relationships can significantly affect the way youngsters react to growing up with a disabled sibling. Crocker (1981) describes a number of potential areas of conflict between parents and children in families with disabled youngsters which may lead to relationship or personal adjustment problems for children.

First, parents may expect their children to accept a special sib-ling as a "normal" family member and emphasize the family's strengths and courage. The children, however, may have a more negative view of the situation and a host of troubled feelings including anxiety and jealousy. Youngsters may possess a secret wish for a "normal" sibling, but may be reluctant to reveal their anxieties and wishes for fear of angering their parents. The par-ents, in turn, may be reluctant to recognize the children's unhap-piness and deny that problems exist.

In addressing such problems, several writers have emphasized the importance of open communication between parents and chil-dren about issues concerning disabled siblings. Some studies suggest that parents may try to protect their children from details about the sibling's welfare or actually deny the implications of the disabling condition themselves (Murphy, Pueschel, Duffy & Brady, 1976; Turk, 1964). Youngsters who grow up feeling free to discuss their sibling's condition, however, seem to develop better coping strategies and may end up being better adjusted (Grossman, 1972). Some youngsters report being particularly concerned about their parents' plans for the disabled siblings' future (Grossman, 1972).

A growing number of programs have been established for siblings of disabled children, ranging from discussion groups, to books for children, and a newsletter for professionals, parents, and siblings. Powell and Ogle (1985) have reviewed a variety of intervention strategies that may be beneficial to these youngsters. An important goal of many efforts seems to be to let youngsters know that their anxieties, anger, feelings of ambivalence and coping problems are normal, and to provide a forum for the expression and exchange of personal experiences.

A second problem noted by Crocker (1981) is that parents may promote the idea that any accomplishment is possible for the disabled sibling and, consequently, expect near-normal interactions and activities between children and their disabled siblings. By contrast, children may feel that they always must be the ones to give in to their sibling's desires and needs, and that their parents do not understand how hard it is to get along with the disabled brother or sister.

One answer to this problem lies in efforts to train children in behavior management strategies so that they feel more effective in handling a difficult sibling (Weinrott, 1974). Children also have been trained to serve as "therapists" for their siblings, an experience which may give the brothers and sisters a sense of pride and comradery in their mutual accomplishments (Lavigueur, 1976; Miller & Cantwell, 1976). In mainstreamed school programs, teachers are encouraged to develop plans for cooperative activities reinforcing to both disabled and nondisabled youngsters (McHale & Gamble, 1986). At home, instructions to "go play with your brother" may be interpreted as requests to babysit or to entertain by school-age children and teens. To promote good feelings between siblings, parents may need to actively plan genuinely and mutually enjoyable sibling and family activities. They also may need to understand the increased need for autonomy and time outside the family that is normal for many youngsters as they approach the teenage years. According to Crocker (1981), parents also should minimize their own preoccupations with the disabled child, and they should not expect other children to be preoccupied with the disabled child's well-being and progress.

Crocker (1981) suggests that another major source of conflict for children is that they often must cope with a double standard in the family for child compliance and rules: the nondisabled child may be expected to adhere to rules for conduct or to perform household responsibilities, but the child with special needs may have a less rigid set of standards. As noted earlier, our own research indicates that children's perceptions of parental "fairness" (how parents treat a child relative to his or her siblings) is an important correlate of children's well-being. Of course, such a correlation cannot tell us whether children's feelings of depression or low self-esteem cause them to see their parents as unfair or whether "unfair" treatment causes children's adjustment problems. Clearly, the ways in which children develop their ideas about parental favoritism need to be investigated more fully. Parents need to be made aware, if they are not already, that children seem very much inclined to make comparisons between parental expectations and treatment of themselves versus their siblings. One area where this may be especially important is in parents' expectations for achievements by their nondisabled children. In some cases, for example, nondisabled children in the family may feel the need to compensate for the limitations of the handicapped sibling by getting high grades in school or excelling in athletic skills (Taylor, 1974). One study found that this pressure seems to be the greatest when there is only one nonhandicapped child in the family (Cleveland & Miller, 1977).

Children may find sibling discussion groups to be a supportive context for expression these feelings which other youngsters share. Parents, on their other part, need to make sure that the disabled child is not unnecessarily dependent or overly indulged, but is making whatever contributions to the family that he or she is capable of making.

A final consideration raised by Crocker (1981) is that the concerns and challenges of rearing a disabled child may have effects on other relationships in the family; they may strengthen family bonds, or conversely, heighten conflict and negativity among family members. Some evidence suggests, for instance, that parents of disabled children may be at risk for marital conflict and divorce (Fotheringham & Creel, 1974; Price-Bonham & Addison, 1978). In our own research, we found that youngsters with disabled siblings, girls in particular, report having more negative interactions with their mothers than do children with nondisabled siblings. The frequency of these negative maternal interactions, in turn, is related to measures of children's well-being. Little attention has been paid to father-child relationships in these families, but some anecdotal information suggests that fathers may cope by becoming distant and uninvolved. From other lines of research, we know that the lack of a close relationship with a father predicts problems with depression and low self-esteem, particularly in adolescent girls (Wallerstein, 1983). Sisters of disabled children may be more vulnerable to depression when they are unable to develop close relationships with their fathers.

SUMMARY AND CONCLUSIONS

Our review of the literature on children with disabled siblings suggests that these youngsters face a special set of challenges in their family lives. These challenges do not seem to manifest themselves in negative feelings or behavior toward their siblings. In fact, these children may treat their siblings more kindly and spend more time caring for them than do children with nondisabled brothers and sisters. Instead children's reactions seem to be more internalized. On the negative side, children may feel more anxious and depressed and have lower self-esteem. These consequences may be more likely when children experience more negativity with their siblings and their mothers or when they see their parents' behavior as unfair. On the positive side, children's experiences may give rise to more mature, other-oriented and humanitarian interests in the long-term. The effects of having a disabled sibling may vary, however, depending on the characteristics of the disabled sibling, the children themselves, and family circumstances.

We have tried to suggest ways parents and professionals can help children cope in more effective ways with problems presented by their disabled siblings. One important strategy involves giving children a chance to talk about their worries, questions, and even their feelings of jealousy or guilt both to parents and to other youngsters who find themselves in a similar situation. Children can also be trained to manage their siblings' behaviors in more appropriate ways, and to manage their own mental and behavioral reactions to problems that rise in day-to-day encounters with their siblings. Finally, parents and professionals can help by better understanding the kinds of problems faced by children growing up with disabled brothers and sisters.

REFERENCES

Bank, S. & Kahn, M. (1982). *The sibling bond*. New York: Basic Books.

Beckman-Bell, P. (1981). Child-related stress in families of handicapped children. *Topics in Early Childhood Special Education, 1*(3), 45-53.

Breslau, N. (1982). Siblings of disabled children: Birth order and age-spacing effects. *Journal of Abnormal Child Psychology, 10*, 85-96.

Bristol, M. M. (1979). *Maternal coping with autistic children: Adequacy of interpersonal support and effect of child's characteristics*. Unpublished doctoral dissertation, University of North Carolina.

Caldwell, B. & Guze, S. (1960). A study of the adjustment of parents and siblings of institutionalized and non-institutionalized retarded children. *American Journal of Mental Deficiency, 64*, 845-855.

Cicirelli, V. A. (1976). Siblings teaching siblings. In V. L. Allen (Ed.), *Children as teachers*. New York: Academic Press.

Cleveland, D. & Miller, N. (1977). Attitudes and life commitment of older siblings of mentally retarded adults: An exploratory study. *Mental Retardation, 3*, 38-41.

Crocker, A. (1981). The involvement of siblings of children with handicaps. In A. Milunsky (Ed.), *Coping with crisis and handicap*. New York: Plenum.

Dunn, J. (1983). Sibling relationships in early childhood. *Child Development, 54*, 787-811.

Elder, G. (1974). *Children of the great depression*. Chicago: University of Chicago Press.

Elkind, D. (1967). Egocentrism in adolescence. *Child Development, 38*, 1025-1034.

Farber, B. (1959). Effects of a severely mentally retarded child on family integration. *Monographs of the Society for Research in Child Development, 24*(2, Serial No. 71).

Farber, B. (1960). Family organization in crisis: Maintenance of integration in families with a severely mentally retarded child. *Monographs of the Society for Research in Child Development, 25*(1, Serial No. 75).

Farber, B. (1964). *Family: Organization and interaction*. San Francisco: Chandler.

Farber, B. & Jenné, W. C. (1963). Family organization and parent-child communication: Parents and siblings of a retarded child. *Monographs of the Society for Research in Child Development, 28*(7, Serial No. 91).

Farber, B. & Ryckman, D. B. (1965). Effects of severely mentally retarded children on family relationships. *Mental Retardation Abstracts, 2*, 1-17.

Fotheringham, J. B. & Creel, D. (1974). Handicapped children and handicapped families. *International Review of Education, 20*, 355-373.

Gamble, W. (1985). *The experiences and coping strategies of children with handicapped and nonhandicapped siblings*. Unpublished doctoral dissertation, The Pennsylvania State University.

Gamble, W., McHale, S. & Ballard, J. (1985, April). *My sister made me do it: Children's attributions about the causes of sibling conflict*. Paper presented at the biennial meeting of the Society for Research in Adolescence, Madison, Wisconsin.

Gath, A. (1972). The mental health of siblings of congenitally abnormal children. *Journal of Child Psychology and Psychiatry, 13*, 211-218.

Gath, A. (1974). Sibling reactions to mental handicap: A comparison of the brothers and sisters of mongol children. *Journal of Child Psychology and Psychiatry, 15*, 187-198.

Gralicker, B. V., Fishler, K. & Koch, R. (1962). Teenage reactions to a mentally retarded sibling. *American Journal of Mental Deficiency, 66*(6), 838-843.

Grossman, F. K. (1972). *Brothers and sisters of retarded children*. Syracuse: Syracuse University Press.

Holroyd, J. & McArthur, D. (1976). Mental retardation and stress on the parents: A contrast between Down's syndrome and childhood autism. *American Journal of Mental Deficiency, 80*, 431-436.

Holt, K. S. (1958). The home care of severely retarded children. *Pediatrics, 22*, 744-755.

Kagan, J. (1983). Perspectives on continuity. In D. Brim & J. Kagan (Eds.), *Constancy and change in human development*. Cambridge, MA: Harvard University Press.

Kaplan, F. (1969). Siblings of the retarded. In S. Sarason & J. Doris (Eds.), *Psychological problems in mental deficiency*. New York: Harper & Row.

Kolin, K., Scherzer, A., New, B. & Garfield, M. (1971). Studies of the school-age child with myelomeningocele: Social and emotional adaptation. *Pediatrics, 78*, 1013-1019.

Lauterbach, C. G. (1974). *Socio-behavioral adaptation of siblings of the mentally handicapped child*. Scranton, PA: The Print Shop.

Lavigne, J. V. & Ryan, M. (1979). Psychologic adjustment of siblings of children with chronic illness. *Pediatrics, 63*, 616-627.

Lavigueur, H. (1976). The use of siblings as an adjunct to the behavioral treatment of children in the home with parents as therapists. *Behavior Therapy, 7*(5), 602-613.

Lloyd-Bostock, S. (1976). Parents' experiences of official help and guidance in caring for a mentally handicapped child. *Child: Care, Health, and Development, 2*, 325-338.

Lonsdale, G. (1978). Family life with a handicapped child: The parents speak. *Child: Care, Health, and Development, 4*, 99-120.

Mash, E. & Mercer, B. (1979). A comparison of the behavior of deviant and nondeviant boys while playing alone and interacting with a sibling. *Journal of Child Psychology and Psychiatry and Allied Disciplines, 20*, 197-207.

McHale, S. & Gamble, W. (1984, April). *Dimensions of sibling relationships of children with handicapped and nonhandicapped siblings*. Paper presented at the biennial meeting of the Society for Research in Child Development, Toronto, Canada.

McHale, S. & Gamble, W. (1986). Mainstreaming handicapped children in public school settings: Challenges and limitations. In E. Schopler & G. Mesibov (Eds.), *Social behavior in autism.* New York: Plenum.

McHale, S. & Gamble, W. (1987). Relationships between handicapped children and their nonhandicapped siblings and peers. In J. Garbarino, T. Brookhauser & K. Authier (Eds.), *Special children – special risks: The maltreatment of handicapped children.* New York: Aldine.

McHale, S., Simeonsson, R. J. & Sloan, J. (1984). Children with handicapped brothers and sisters. In E. Schopler & G. Mesibov (Eds.), *Issues in autism, Vol. 2. The effects of autism on the family* (pp. 327-342). New York: Plenum.

McHale, S., Sloan, J. & Simeonsson, R. J. (1986). Sibling relationships with autistic, mentally retarded, and nonhandicapped brothers and sisters: A comparative study. *Journal of Autism and Developmental Disorders, 16,*399-414.

Meichenbaum, D. (1977). *Cognitive behavior modification: An integrative approach.* New York: Plenum.

Miller, N. & Cantwell, D. (1976). Siblings as therapists: A behavioral approach. *American Journal of Psychiatry, 133,* 447-450.

Miller, S. G. (1974). An exploratory study of sibling relationships in families with retarded children. *Dissertation Abstracts International, 35,* 74-26, 606.

Murphy, A., Pueschel, S., Duffy, T. & Brady, E. (1976). Meeting with brothers and sisters of children with Down's Syndrome. *Children Today, 5,* 20-23.

Ogle, P. (1982). *The sibling relationship: Maternal perceptions of the nonhandicapped and handicapped/nonhandicapped dyads.* Unpublished doctoral dissertation, University of North Carolina at Chapel Hill.

O'Neill, J. (1965). Siblings of the retarded. Individual counseling. *Children, 12,* 226-229.

Peltz, L. (1977). *An exploratory study of the interactional behavior of psychotic children with psychotic peers and normal siblings.* Unpublished doctoral dissertation, Columbia University.

Powell, T. & Ogle, P. (1985). *Brothers and sisters: A special part of exceptional families.* Baltimore: Paul H. Brookes.

Price-Bonham, S. & Addison, S. (1978). Families with mentally retarded children: Emphases on the father. *The Family Coordinator, 3,* 221-230.

Samuels, H. R. (1980). The effect of an older sibling on infant locomotor exploration of a new environment. *Child Development, 51,* 607-609.

San Martino, M. & Newman, M. (1974). Siblings of retarded children: A population at risk. *Child Psychiatry and Human development, 4,* 168-177.

Schreiber, M. & Feeley, M. (1965). Siblings of the retarded: A guided group experience. *Children, 12,* 221-225.

Shaeffer, E. & Edgerton, M. (1981). *The sibling inventory of behavior.* Unpublished manuscript, University of North Carolina, Chapel Hill.

Stoneman, Z. & Brody, G. H. (1984). Research with families of severely handicapped children: Theoretical and methodological considerations. In J. Blacher (Ed.), *Severely handicapped young children and their families: Research in review.* New York: Academic Press.

Taylor, L. S. (1974). *Communication between mothers and normal siblings of retarded children: Nature and modification.* Unpublished dissertation, University of North Carolina.

Tew, B. & Laurence, K. M. (1973). Mothers, brothers, and sisters of patients with spina bifida. *Developmental Medicine Child Neurology, 15,* 69-76.

Turk, J. (1964). Impact of cystic fibrosis on family functioning. *Pediatrics, 34,* 67.

Wallerstein, J. S. (1983). Children of divorce: Stress and developmental tasks. In N. Garmezy and M. Rutter (Eds.), *Stress, coping, and development in children*. New York: McGraw-Hill.

Weinrott, M. R. (1974). A training program in behavior modification for siblings of the retarded. *American Journal of Orthopsychiatry, 44*, 362-375.

Wikler, L. (1983). Chronic stresses of families of mentally retarded children. *Family Relations, 30*, 281-288.

Zuk, G., Miller, R., Bertram, J. & Kling, F. (1961). Maternal acceptance of retarded children: A questionnaire study of attitudes and religious backgrounds. *Child Development, 32*, 525-540.

Siblings of the Child with a Life-Threatening Illness

Barbara M. Sourkes, PhD

SUMMARY. This paper examines the experience of siblings who live with a child with a life-threatening illness, and the adaptive means they mobilize to negotiate this unique life stress. The author highlights the themes which have emerged from her psychotherapeutic work with siblings by the children's statements and drawings, and stipulates intervention strategies. Key issues in bereavement are also discussed. The siblings' experience must be seen within a "normalized" framework at the juncture of three perspectives: the family system; a focus on life rather than on death; and a view to positive adaptation.

It's no privilege having someone with cancer in your family. Of all the things I ever could have chosen, having my brother get cancer is not one of them.

Sourkes, 1982

    This paper examines the experience of siblings of the pediatric cancer patient, both in living with the illness, and in bereavement. The focus is on the issues which the siblings face, and the adaptive means they mobilize to negotiate this unique life stress. The clinical data presented may be extrapolated to siblings of children with other life-threatening diseases.

Barbara M. Sourkes is Associate in Psychology, The Children's Hospital, and Instructor in Psychology in the Department of Psychiatry, Harvard Medical School, Boston, MA. Mailing address: 40-A St. Paul Street, Brookline, MA 02146.

This is a revised and updated version of the chapter "Siblings of the Pediatric Cancer Patient" which appeared in: J. Kellerman (Ed.), *Psychological Aspects of Childhood Cancer*, 1980. Courtesy of Charles C Thomas, Publisher, Springfield, IL.

REVIEW OF PREVIOUS LITERATURE

As a result of medical advances, the focus of the literature has shifted from "the bereaved sibling" or "the sibling of the dying child" to the "the sibling of the child with a chronic/life-threatening illness." Although the threat of separation and death remains omnipresent, it is now necessary to study siblings' experience of living with an ill child over a prolonged period. Another shift has been from a focus on psychopathology and disturbance in the siblings to positive adaptation. The initial psychiatric studies highlighted the extremes of siblings' problems but gave little sense of the continuum of coping. Many studies were retrospective, with a built-in temporal distortion, or depended exclusively on parental reports, often including a negative bias. Early studies dealt mostly with siblings of leukemia patients, or, in some articles, the specific diagnosis is not named. It is becoming evident that different forms of malignant disease may have differing impact on the siblings. Whereas, the initial literature questioned the costs and benefits of telling the diagnosis, the crucial focus now is: What is the impact on siblings of living with the knowledge of the patient's life-threatening illness?

In a pioneering study, Cain, Fast, and Erickson (1964) investigated children's disturbed reactions to the death of a sibling. They reviewed the psychiatric files of 58 children whose symptoms had been attributed to the death of a sibling. Their reactions affected both cognitive and emotional functioning on multiple levels: intrapsychic, family, peer, neighborhood, school, and community. The major negative factor for many of these siblings was parental unavailability during hospitalizations and then during the mourning period.

Binger, Ablin, Feuerstein, Kushner, Zoger, and Mikkelsen (1969) and Binger (1973) were among the first to study the difficulties of siblings of pediatric leukemia patients. In a retrospective study of 20 families who had lost a child, in half the families at least one sibling had shown evidence of difficulty during the illness. Symptoms included enuresis, headaches, abdominal pain, school problems, depression and separation anxiety, often accompanied by feelings of rejection, guilt and fear. The authors stress the necessity for attention to siblings both as prevention and intervention.

Lindsay and MacCarthy (1974) present issues within a developmental framework. They state that the infant sibling is at highest risk because crucial early bonding may be disrupted by the mother's preoccupation with an ill child. The toddler, too young for comprehensive verbal explanation, may interpret parental preoccupation as rejection, and show regression in development. The school-aged sibling feels a complex of resentment, anger, and guilt in addition to the rejection, and must learn to cope with the elevated anxiety within the family. Negative behavior, poor school performance, withdrawal and psychosomatic symptoms may result. The authors point out the ebb and flow nature of the parents' preoccupation with the sick child. The highest intensity appears at the time of diagnosis, during relapses, or during exacerbations of the illness. The loss of confidence in parenting skills once a child is ill may generalize to feeling inadequate with the siblings as well.

Wiener (1970) lists the factors which influence the reaction of siblings to the fatal illness of a child. Included are: sibling age and maturity; ability to integrate the meaning of the illness; relationship to the patient; place and adjustment in the family; honesty of communication; and how the sibling is involved in the family adaptation to crisis.

Share (1972) discusses the meaning of the illness to the well siblings. She stresses that siblings lose customary attention both by the parents' physical absence as well as by the emotional realignments which occur within the family. Valued family routines and activities are changed. The siblings are angry at the parents and competitive toward the ill child. Most of the anger toward the patient will surface while the child is in remission. The siblings may then be overcome by guilt and fear during the patient's hospitalization.

Kagen-Goodheart (1977) focuses on the problems of living with childhood cancer. When the patient comes home from the hospital, the siblings are confronted with an extremely difficult transition; they expect all to be as before; and yet, it is not. The siblings must be prepared for the fact that the patient will require extra attention even at home. Kagen-Goodheart (1977) makes a critical point not mentioned in most articles: the patient may express anger toward the siblings for being well.

Townes and Wold (1977) studied 22 siblings of eight leukemia patients. Their overall finding was that the siblings' evaluation of the patient's disease as life-threatening was related to increased parental communication about the implications of the disease and the experience of living with the disease over time.

Gogan, Koocher, Foster, and O'Malley (1977) assessed 13 siblings of long-term survivors of pediatric cancer. The investigators found that the siblings' understanding of the patient's potential fatality increased as a function of present age and age at diagnosis. Most siblings minimized the impact of the illness at the time it had occurred. None claimed to remember feeling abandoned. While some rivalry was described, little guilt was expressed. Most siblings said that the patient had changed as a result of the illness, but denied change in themselves.

Lavigne and Ryan (1979) compared siblings of pediatric hematology (leukemia and solid tumor), cardiology and plastic surgery patients with siblings of healthy children on the Louisville Behavior Checklist (filled out by parent). Siblings of all three categories of ill children were significantly more withdrawn and irritable than siblings of well children. In children ages 7 to 13 years, brothers of hematology patients showed significantly more symptoms than sisters. There were no group differences in aggression or learning problems. Lavigne and Ryan (1979) conclude that there is not a point-to-point correspondence between severity of illness and degree of behavioral problems, and that perhaps under increased stress, siblings develop better coping skills.

Cairns, Clark, Smith and Lansky (1979) used three assessment scales to compare the adjustment of school-aged cancer patients and their siblings in 71 families. Findings demonstrated that the siblings showed even more distress than the patients in perceived social isolation, fear of the expression of negative feelings within the family, the perception of parents as being overly attentive to the ill child, and concern about failure (older siblings only). Both the patients and siblings expressed similar levels of anxiety about illness and injury. The authors discuss the reactive stress, not pathology, of the siblings as empirical validation of many clinical impressions.

A three-year longitudinal study by Spinetta and Deasy-Spinetta (1981) is the first to examine systematically the entire family's response to childhood cancer. Using psychological tests, they found that siblings suffer as much as, and at times more than, the patient with regard to not having emotional needs met within the family. In the four- to six-year range, siblings showed less adaptive coping than patients, lower self-concept, and were more sensitive to the patients than vice-versa. They also saw their parents as being more distant from them than did patients. In the six- to twelve-year-old group, the siblings' adaptation scores decreased as the patients' pain increased, as both patients and parents, however, showed improved communication and emotional coping at these times. The siblings also scored poorly when the families as a whole were doing relatively well. The authors point out that siblings "seem to lose out on both ends" (p. 140). During crisis, all parental attention is focused on the patient, and when the patient improves, parental concerns shift to non-disease related matters, and the siblings are again left without support.

A study from the family-systems literature (Koch, 1985) used interview schedules for siblings and parents of 32 pediatric cancer patients. Two crucial factors emerged: how family rules permit or prohibit emotional expression, and how roles change as a result of the illness. Preventive interventions include: teaching family members how to disclose feelings in a nonthreatening way, and the normalization of emotions and of role changes when a family is faced with childhood cancer.

Bank and Kahn (1982) include a chapter on "siblings as survivors" in their book on sibling relationships. They discuss both short- and long-term consequences of losing a sibling during childhood, adolescence or early adulthood. Two crucial factors are cited: the model of grieving that the parents present, and the type of identification which existed between the children while the sibling was alive. They point out that the circumstances of the death (its horror, the duration of the dying, the possibility of prevention, and the age of the surviving sibling) may have differing ramifications. "The dead sibling's legacy can be a force for sickness and stagnation or . . . can serve as an inspiration for maturation and creativity" (p. 271).

Excellent literature reviews have been compiled by McKeever (1983) and Drotar and Crawford (1985). The authors emphasize that while serious chronic or life-threatening illness in a child is a family stressor, psychopathology and severe maladjustment among siblings is not a necessary consequence. Drotar and Crawford (1985) point out that the quality of the marital and the sibling relationships are important mediators. As research begins to be guided by a "competency" model, rather than by a disease/deficit-centered perspective, a more balanced view of the siblings will evolve.

LIVING WITH CHILDHOOD CANCER

What are the normal and expected concerns of siblings of the child with a life-threatening illness? Many questions and issues are ubiquitous although the mode of expression may depend upon the child's cognitive and emotional developmental stage. Some reactions which initially seem disruptive may in fact represent an adaptation to a unique life stress. The concerns raised by the siblings do not begin and end at specific points in the illness of the patient. Rather, in an ebb and flow fashion, they will recede or resurge in importance at different times. In the same way that normal stages and reactions are acknowledged in the patient's adaption, so the siblings' experience must be seen from a "normalized" perspective.

In the following section, themes which have emerged from my psychotherapeutic work with pediatric cancer patients and their siblings will be described. The children's own statements and drawings illustrate their concerns most aptly. The intervention strategies can be a means for facilitating communication with siblings either by a therapist or by parents and other caregivers. The thematic categories are neither mutually exclusive, nor are they necessarily an exhaustive list. They can, however, provide a foundation for further exploration.

Causation of the Illness

Siblings often hold two views about the cause of the patient's illness. One view stems from the medical information which they have heard from their parents and the doctors. The other is their own "private" version, often unarticulated, but to which they cling with tenacity. Their private cause is often fraught with emotional and cognitive confusion. From a cognitive point of view, causality is a difficult concept for young children to grasp. They often construe simultaneity, or unrelated sequence of events, as comprising a cause-effect relationship. Combined with intense emotional factors of fear or guilt, the siblings' thinking often contains magical links as their way to make sense of something overwhelming and incomprehensible. Children, like adults, will supply a cause to fill in the gaps when knowledge is lacking or not fully grasped. Their view of the cause often becomes an undergirding theme in their experience of the patient's illness.

Following are siblings' responses to the question: "What do you think caused your brother's/sister's illness? What made him/her sick?"

She fell off the slide and broke her arm.

(Cliff, 6; brother of Susan, 13, osteogenic sarcoma)

He got sick because I had a sore throat and he caught it.

(Five-year-old sister of twelve-year-old leukemic patient)

He had a temperature. He's sick. He's not better yet. He's almost better.

(Ken, 4; brother of Brad, 2, leukemia)

She had hurt her leg on the chain of her bike. She didn't even notice it until I pointed it out to her. I don't even ride my bike anymore. One night I went out and broke the chain so I couldn't ride it. I told my mother it broke by itself, but I broke it.

(Bobby, 10; brother of Cindy, 14, osteogenic sarcoma)

In each of these examples, the siblings have supplied a reason which is either coexistent with a medical view or other than a medical view. The self-references in their explanations are of crucial importance.

The critical intervention is to obtain the sibling's version of the cause of the disease. The sooner this view is obtained, the more quickly misconceptions can be clarified. Most children will be pleased, and relieved, to share their reasoning. It will be important to reiterate the medical view many times during the illness, and to be vigilant for the reemergence of any guilt associated with the child's initial reasoning.

With young children who have cognitive difficulty with causality, basic help with that concept in general may help them to understand the illness situation in specific. In everyday situations, a child can be shown that simultaneity or sequence does not necessarily imply cause. They may then better understand the relative randomness of the patient's illness within a complex of other occurrences.

If the sibling is restricting himself or herself from an activity out of fear, clarifying explanations or a desensitization approach may facilitate its resumption.

Visibility of the Illness and the Treatment Process

An issue rarely mentioned in the literature, but which emerged repeatedly in discussions with the siblings, is the effect of the visibility or the invisibility of the disease. This factor plays a particularly important role in the initial period after diagnosis. An illness which leads to a dramatic physical change such as an amputation provides a visible focus for explanation. Yet, the siblings may grapple with whether or not the patient is still the same person, despite the altered appearance. Young siblings may be puzzled by the invisibility of a disease like leukemia and supply their own real and imagined symptoms. Loss of hair and weight become visual cues in most illnesses; however, the effect is less enduring than that of an amputation.

The visibility or invisibility of the treatment process is a related issue. Siblings may perceive the hospital and clinic as threatening places, or, they may envy "outings" to the clinic, resenting the patient's chance for time with the parents, and resenting the patient's missing school. They may not understand that although "treatment" is a word with positive valence, the procedures, in actuality, can be dreadful and painful. In the absence of experience, an integrated understanding is difficult for the siblings to achieve.

The following examples illustrate the interweaving of the visibility/invisibility of the disease with the treatment process. In the first vignette, a child tries to "make visible" what is invisible and mysterious.

> Ken drew a picture of Brad, saying: "This is Brad with broken legs and a broken mouth. He has a broken dead face and a booboo mouth. What happens if Brad is dead? Like he got run over when a car comes?" Once Ken had seen Brad in the hospital, he reported: "I saw Brad. He was crying. He was bald. I saw him when he had hair."
>
> (Ken, 4; brother of Brad, 2, leukemia)

In the following vignette, the impact of amputation of visible illness is highlighted.

> Bobby wrote the following story: "This is my sister (drew a one-legged stick figure) and this is me (drew a two-legged figure). There is a difference. But I still think that this is the same Cindy, and I know that she is not the same to you, and I think that she is beautiful." He then drew a picture of Cindy, stressing her very short hair, and her stump. (See Figure 1.) He expressed much concern about how her stump would look.
>
> (Bobby, 10; brother of Cindy, 14, osteogenic sarcoma)

The siblings' task is to coordinate the concepts of constancy and change, sameness and difference. They must learn that it is the same person who looks so different, or that despite constancy in appearance, inner change is making the child ill.

Drawings are helpful in working with young siblings. How the child portrays the patient, whether the changes in appearance are included or omitted, provides a basis for discussion. It is also interesting to compare this drawing with a sibling's self-portrait. In an "invisible" disease such as leukemia, simplified illustrations (of the types of blood cells, for example) can be invaluable for explanation.

Siblings' visits to the hospital and clinic are critical in demystifying the treatment process. In seeing other patients and siblings, they develop a context for their own experience.

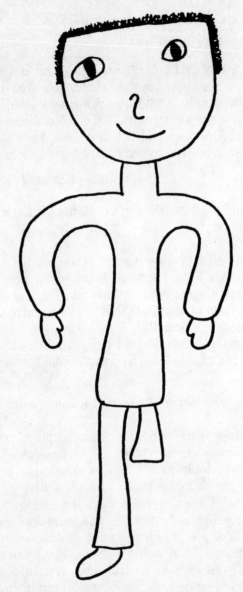

FIGURE 1. Bobby's picture of Cindy.

Identification with the Illness

The fear of taking ill with cancer runs high among a sibling group. There is ample reason for this frightening identification. The siblings see many similarities between themselves and the patient. As children in the same family, past experiences that affected one child often affected another. Thus, it is only a matter of extension that an illness which could befall one child could just as easily befall another. This logic is especially true when the siblings cannot stipulate, either cognitively or emotionally, a cause for the illness. The apparent randomness of events leads the sibling to think: "Why not me too?"

> When Bobby was asked if he has any fears or nightmares, he replied: "That my leg will get cut off also. I think about it a lot. I wake up and go into the kitchen. All the time I worry about it." (See Figure 2.)
>
> (Bobby, 10; brother of Cindy, 14, osteogenic sarcoma)
>
> Ken described his drawing: "A big rock falls on two boys. They get hurt and bleed and get dead."
>
> (Ken, 4; brother of Brad, 2, leukemia)

The siblings need reassurance that there is little likelihood of their getting the same disease nor is the illness contagious. In order to prevent an overidentification with the patient, siblings must be enabled to pursue their own day-to-day activities and relationships. This independent aspect of their life counterbalances the compelling sense of similarity and identification implied in a sibling relationship.

Guilt and Shame

The siblings' sense of guilt is multifaceted. As seen earlier, many of their views on what caused the patient's illness include either an implicit or explicit self-reference. Beyond the issue of causation, siblings at times feel guilty that they escaped the disease. Acknowledging their relief at being healthy only triggers the guilt more intensely. These children often feel badly when

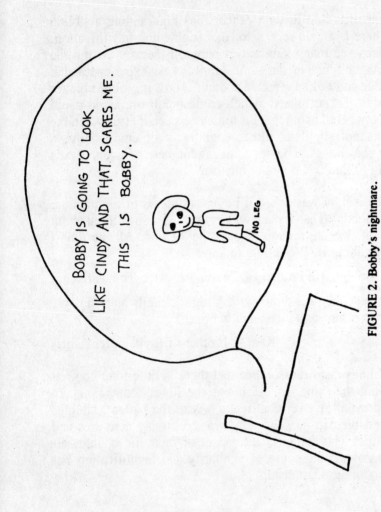

FIGURE 2. Bobby's nightmare.

From Sourkes, B., Siblings of the pediatric cancer patient. In *Psychological Aspects of Childhood Cancer* (p. 59), edited by J. Kellerman, 1980, Springfield, Illinois: Charles C Thomas. Copyright 1980 by Charles C Thomas. Reprinted by permission.

the patient is unable to participate in a particular activity or event because of the illness.

The siblings' guilt can be stirred up from another source: their sense of shame. Rarely mentioned, but often lurking, is the siblings' shame at having a child in the family who is ill, disfigured, and dying. The patient marks the family as "different." Siblings may attribute their shame either to themselves or to the patient; in both cases, the unacceptable feeling only increases the preexistent guilt.

The following statement typifies the siblings' sense of guilt:

> Why didn't I get sick instead of Cindy. I wish it had been me. I don't like to see her hurt.
>
> (Bobby, 10; brother of Cindy, 14, osteogenic sarcoma)

These vignettes illustrate aspects of the shame:

> Ken went through a period of hiding from people saying: "I don't want people to look at me. They will laugh at me." His explanation was somewhat garbled, but it did involve Brad.
>
> (Ken, 4; brother of Brad, 2, leukemia)

> Bobby had originally written his story about Cindy and himself at school (see preceding section *Visibility of the Illness and the Treatment Process*). He reported: "I threw it out because another kid read it." Bobby often talked about how embarrassed Cindy would be to go swimming, because "everyone would say things about her because of the amputation."
>
> (Bobby, 10; brother of Cindy, 14, osteogenic sarcoma)

The siblings need the opportunity to discuss feelings of guilt or shame privately with their parents or another adult close to them. It is also important to ensure that siblings do not constrict their activities out of guilt that the patient cannot participate with them.

Siblings and Their Parents

The mother of a hospitalized patient reported having seen a car bumpersticker which read: "Have you hugged your child today?" She said that the slogan jolted her into realizing how little time she had spent with the siblings at home.

This vignette illustrates a critical issue between siblings of a patient and their parents: attention and nurturance. A pervasive complaint of the siblings is the diminished attention from their parents, especially when the patient is in the hospital. At these times, the parents may be both physically and emotionally unavailable to the children at home. Older siblings who themselves are feeling deprived may resent stepping in as "surrogate parents" for the younger children. The issue is often symbolized in siblings' concern about food, in physical symptoms, and in their need for reassurance about being loved.

Three well siblings in one family all complained that whenever the patient was in the hospital, their mother didn't have time to cook. All they ate were T.V. dinners. Bobby was overheard talking to himself: "Maybe if I catch a cold, Mom will stay home with me more."

(Bobby, 10; brother of Cindy, 14, osteogenic sarcoma)

Ken's parents had been at the hospital with Brad since early morning. When they called home that evening, Ken reported matter-of-factly: "I have something bad to tell you. Carl (the other well sibling) is bald and you had better come home right way."

(Ken, 4; brother of Brad, 2, leukemia)

An eight-year-old sibling of a leukemia patient has appeared to be coping well throughout the four years of her sister's illness. However, she constantly leaves notes for her parents that say "I love you."

When the patient is home, whether ill or in remission, the siblings' complaint shifts slightly from that of "too little attention" to "preferential treatment of the patient." The parents are struggling concurrently: how to maintain equality and normality when, in fact, there is a distinctly "abnormal" factor in the family constellation. Parents may, at least initially, find it difficult to punish the patient; whereas, disciplinary measures for the well siblings remain in effect.

> Bobby drew a picture showing how his mother treated him differently from Cindy. Mother yells at Bobby: "You'd better not touch that fruit." To Cindy, she says: "Please do not touch." After Bobby drew the picture, he smiled, seemingly in relief, and asked if he could draw the picture again — bigger this time! (See Figure 3.)
>
> (Bobby, 10; brother of Cindy, 14, osteogenic sarcoma)

A painful issue is the siblings' anger at the parents for not having been able to protect the patient from the illness. Parents may be perceived as having played a role in the occurrence of the illness. Young siblings may come to this conclusion through a magical juxtaposition of events. Older siblings may wonder why the parents didn't check the patient's symptoms earlier, echoing the parents' own self-questioning. The siblings are shaken by having a life-threatening illness strike so close, and insecure in the parents' ability to protect them.

> Just before Brad's diagnosis of leukemia, the family dog had been given away. While Brad was in the hospital, Ken accused his mother of "lying" to him: "The dog is really dead." He also stated explicitly: "Brad is sick in the hospital. My mother drove him in there."
>
> (Ken, 4; brother of Brad, 2, leukemia)

It is important that the siblings express their concerns about the relationship with their parents. While some siblings may mention only the general decrease in attention (if even that), others may indicate specific complaints such as disorganized meals, or missing favorite activities. Their concerns may change over time and circumstance. Once informed, the parents can mobilize their own

FIGURE 3. How Bobby's mother treats him differently from Cindy.

From Sourkes, B., Siblings of the pediatric cancer patient. In *Psychological Aspects of Childhood Cancer* (p. 61), edited by J. Kellerman, 1980, Springfield, Illinois: Charles C Thomas. Copyright 1980 by Charles C Thomas. Reprinted by permission.

priorities and commitments more effectively. Siblings need regular times alone with one or both parents for sharing feelings and thoughts, and for assurance that they will be "protected" to the parents' optimum capacity. Older siblings should not be pushed into a "surrogate parent" role, even if they have assumed such responsibility in the past. During the patient's illness, other caregivers' support should be enlisted for the younger siblings. It is important, however, to recognize that for some children, their "parenting" duties can be a means of assuaging their own sense of helplessness.

Academic and Social Functioning

The siblings' concern with the patient's illness often affects two areas of daily functioning: school and peer relationships. Siblings' academic performance may be impaired because of their preoccupation, or they may focus on school to assure a sense of competence in the face of stress and helplessness.

> When asked whether he worries during the day about having his leg cut off, Bobby responded solemnly: "I think about it so much. Sometimes the teacher is giving out papers, and I don't hear what she tells us to do because I'm so busy thinking and then she yells at me." During this same period, Bobby insistently requested tutoring in certain subjects, saying that his poor schoolwork was his worst problem.

> (Bobby, 10; brother of Cindy, 14, osteogenic sarcoma)

> Ken had a temper tantrum upon arrival at nursery school. Once calm, he explained that he didn't want to come to school that day because: "I had to go to work to take care of a very sick baby."

> (Ken, 4; brother of Brad, 2, leukemia)

With regard to peer relationships, siblings may curtail contact in their need for a family focus, or they may turn increasingly to their friends for support.

Ken had all the children in his class write their names on a card to Brad, so that: "All my friends will know Brad and Brad will know all my friends."

(Ken, 4; brother of Brad, 2, leukemia)

School and peer relationships represent the ongoing "normal" part of the siblings' lives. They are areas which provide opportunity for mastery, support, and for distance from the illness experience. Teachers must be made aware of the family situation, and consultation must be available to them should siblings manifest problems in the classroom. Parents must maintain and encourage the siblings' peer activities.

Somatic Reactions

Somatic reactions, whether they be actual physical symptoms, sleep problems, or accident proneness, are commonly found within a sibling group. The symptoms may develop as a means of getting parental attention, or the siblings' preoccupation with the patient may lead to carelessness about themselves. In other instances, the symptoms represent symbolically a psychological process which the sibling is experiencing at the time.

Cliff began to bed wet nightly during Susan's prolonged hospitalization. The mother thought that the enuresis was his means of delaying her daily departures to the hospital, since she would wash and change his linen before leaving (Sourkes, 1977).

(Cliff, 6; brother of Susan, 13, osteogenic sarcoma)

As Susan became more emaciated, Jane gained more and more weight. Jane articulated that "getting skinny means that you are dying," and so she kept eating.

(Jane, 11; sister of Susan, 13, osteogenic sarcoma)

Helping siblings to understand the psychological meaning behind the somatic concerns may relieve them of the necessity for psychosomatic expression.

Bidirectionality of the Sibling-Patient Relationship

A bidirectional focus on the sibling-patient relationship is critical within a systems view of the family. The relationship is always a two-way process, regardless of how skewed the balance may be because of one child's illness. Within the reciprocal system of the well sibling and the patient, the predominant themes of mutual anger/resentment and mutual protectiveness/caring emerge.

Siblings may resent the extra attention and privileges accorded the patient, while simultaneously feeling guilty about being healthy. The patient, angry to be sick, resents the siblings for escaping the illness. The patient's anger at the siblings, rarely mentioned in the literature, can be quite devastating for the other children.

> Katy asked her mother: "Why is Frank always so healthy and I'm so sick all the time" Frank overheard her question, and when he couldn't sleep that night, called his mother into his room to "have a talk." In exact reverse, he asked: "Why am I so healthy and Katy so sick?" Katy's resentment was graphically expressed in her family drawing. She drew only her parents and Frank, saying upon questioning that she "forgot" to put herself into the picture. When asked to add herself, she, with forethought, drew herself on top of Frank's head.
>
> (Frank, 4; brother of Katy, 8, leukemia)

> Susan resented that when she was home, Jane spent much time out with friends. Jane was angry that during periods of Susan's hospitalization, she hardly saw her peers because of babysitting responsibilities at home. Susan felt guilty for making demands on Jane's time; Jane, for not abiding more by her sister's wishes.
>
> (Jane, 11; sister of Susan, 13, osteogenic sarcoma)

Given the problem-oriented perspective of the clinical literature, it is not surprising that the positive caring between the patient and siblings has been overlooked. To ignore this reciprocity is to neglect the children's most adaptive means of coping.

> Ken was proud to bring a candy to Brad in the hospital. In his therapy sessions, Ken would pretend to be a doctor taking care of baby Brad. When Brad was home again and the family was at a restaurant, Ken overheard another child laughing at Brad's baldness. Ken immediately went up to the child and said: "If you say anything bad about my baby brother I'll punch you. He is bald because he is sick."

> (Ken, 4; brother of Brad, 2, leukemia)

> Susan's explanation for her sister's infrequent visits to the hospital was: "Jane is afraid to see me without any hair and looking so sick, although I wish she would come more often." Jane thought that Susan was ashamed to be seen, and in fact wanted to visit more (Sourkes, 1977).

> (Jane, 11; sister of Susan, 13, osteogenic sarcoma)

> Karen (patient) said to the therapist: "Please could you go and talk to my sister *alone*. She needs someone to talk to. Please do it as a favor to me."

> (Karen, 13, leukemia)

The most critical task for the therapist is to facilitate communication between the patient and siblings. It is important to know what the relationship was like before the illness, as a baseline for understanding change. Parents can be encouraged to observe the sibling relationship and to help the children broach problems as they arise. At times, joint sessions with the patient and sibling can be of profound impact.

DEATH OF THE PATIENT AND BEREAVEMENT OF THE SIBLINGS

With the death of the patient, the siblings suffer multiple losses: the patient himself or herself, and then all the roles which were inherent in the relationship. While the patient is alive, a huge amount of time and energy is invested in that person as the center of the family constellation. When the person dies, much reordering must occur as part of the family's readaptation process.

Children's mode of expression varies from adults' in many life situations. Thus, it is not surprising that their grieving may be different, although no less valid, than the adult process. In psychotherapeutic work with bereaved siblings, the aim is to make the covert more overt in their mourning. Verbal interaction, drawing and dollhouse play are all means of inducing expression.

At home, there are two central issues during the acute bereavement period. First, is the question of the siblings' attendance at the funeral. If parents discuss the issue directly with the siblings, then they can often make a decision based upon the children's direct or indirect cues. No child should ever be forced to attend. Secondly, while it is important to talk about the deceased child, the here-and-how life focus of the well siblings should also be stressed. This is a critical period to ensure prevention of insidious comparison with the idealized dead child, or the beginning of a replacement child process.

In the replacement child process, parents project many of the attributes (both positive and negative) and responsibilities of the dead child onto a surviving sibling. This chosen child is often of the same sex, or nearest in age to the child who died. For this child, the issues around differentiation of identity, already complicated by a sibling death, can build into overriding confusion: Who *was* I before my brother/sister's death? Who *am* I now? A replacement child process, whether insidious or overt, can dangerously preclude the possibility of the healing of bereavement within the entire family.

In the following examples of siblings' mourning, note the interplay of conventional verbal reminiscence with the more concrete working through of younger children. The description of Frank's reactions (age 4) to Katy's death (age 8, leukemia) was obtained from the parents in follow-up interview and phone calls.

> When Frank was told of Katy's death, he immediately said that he wished he had had the chance to say goodbye. Over the next few days, he asked many questions: Why was Katy dead; what did dead mean; what did she look like now? The parents told Frank that although Katy could no longer talk to

him, he could still tell her things if it would make him feel better. During the first month after Katy's death, Frank asked to go to the cemetery several times. At the grave, he would pose questions to Katy through his mother; for example, "Ask Katy if she really loved me." He would recount anecdotes to Katy about his life, such as his first day of nursery school. When the family dog was found after being lost for a day, Frank insisted on going to the cemetery with the dog so that Katy would know about his return! In school, Frank immediately attached himself to a little girl in his class, and would panic on days she was absent. About a month after Katy died, while Frank was in the bathtub, he suddenly burst into sobs about how much he missed taking a bath with Katy. Evidently bathtime continued to be difficult for about six months, but eventually it became a time for happy recollection about the bath games he and Katy used to play together. Almost a year later, Frank still wakes up some mornings and says that he feels sad because he misses his sister.

What are the instructive points to be garnered from the description of Frank's mourning process? First, in Frank's wish to say goodbye to Katy, his understanding of the finality of death can be seen. His intellectualized questions about death are an adaptive form of cognitive mastery of a highly abstract concept. Through his "talking to Katy," Frank could begin to understand that although she was no longer alive, he could continue to remember her. Frank's immediate attachment to the girl at school represents the concrete replacement so often seen in young siblings along with their heightened sensitivity to the threat of loss. Frank's bathtime reminiscences are similar to adult grieving when memories are stirred up by activities once shared. Frank's expressed sadness on waking some mornings is a spontaneous form of grieving, and in no way induced by adult probing.

An older child's concerns are illustrated in therapeutic sessions with Bobby (10 years), following the death of Cindy (14 years).

When asked about the funeral, Bobby responded that it had been "scary" to see Cindy's body. He noted that she looked "cold and bigger." On the therapist's suggestion, he drew a picture of her in the casket, carefully adding a necklace charm which said "I love you." He had given her this necklace before Christmas. It was suggested that Bobby write a letter to Cindy, telling her anything that felt "unfinished." He wrote: "To Cindy. I wish you would be here to see how I feel. Cindy, I wish you could come home to stay with me forever and ever. I miss going bowling with you. Love, Bobby." After he had read the letter aloud, the therapist asked him if he could further specify how he feels, using the sentence cue: "I feel . . . " Bobby wrote: "I feel like a bug is just eating me up." He then drew a picture of a boy with bugs "in the leg and chest only" — the sites of Cindy's cancer. (See Figure 4.)

The expression of Bobby's grieving was induced through talking, drawing and writing. Bobby's initial comment about his fright at seeing Cindy's body set the stage for candor throughout the sessions. Like many children, his focus on the sense impressions of seeing Cindy ("cold and bigger") was interwoven with the fear. Bobby's continuing feeling for Cindy was represented in the "I love you" necklace she wore. He expressed his missing Cindy both in general terms, and with specific reference to a favorite shared activity. In Bobby's drawing of the bug eating him up is illustrated the identification with Cindy through the illness sites, and the power of his grief. The drawing of the child after death, the letter stating "unfinished" concerns, and the "I feel . . . " sentence cue, are all valuable techniques in working with bereaved siblings.

These children are unusually expressive with parents who facilitated their openness throughout the illness-death process. These siblings, however, articulate what all children are thinking and the opportunity for their mourning must be provided.

CONCLUSIONS

Clinical and research data on siblings of the child with a life-threatening illness have been presented. The siblings' experience may be seen at the juncture of three perspectives: the family system; a focus on living rather than on dying; and a view toward positive adaptation rather than psychopathology. The most criti-

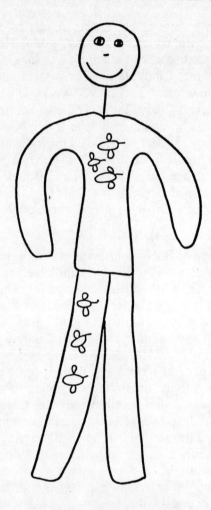

IT FEELS LIKE A BUG JUST
EATING ME UP. THE BUGS
ARE ONLY IN MY LEG AND
CHEST.

FIGURE 4. How Bobby feels after Cindy's death.

From Sourkes, B., Siblings of the pediatric cancer patient. In *Psychological Aspects of Childhood Cancer* (p. 67), edited by J. Kellerman, 1980, Springfield, Illinois: Charles C Thomas. Copyright 1980 by Charles C Thomas. Reprinted by permission.

cal focus is on the sibling-patient relationship itself. The strengths inherent and unique to this relationship are enriching, and they can facilitate the growth of the entire family.

REFERENCES

Bank, S. & Kahn, M. (1981). *The sibling bond.* New York: Basic Books.

Binger, C. (1973). Childhood leukemia – emotional impact on siblings. In E. J. Anthony & C. Koupernik (Eds.), *The child in his family: The impact of disease and death* (pp. 195-210). New York: John Wiley and Sons.

Binger, C., Ablin, A., Feuerstein, R., Kushner, J., Zoger, S. & Mikkelsen, C. (1969). Childhood leukemia: Emotional impact on patient and family. *The New England Journal of Medicine, 280,* 414-418.

Cain, A., Fast, I. & Erickson, M. (1964). Children's disturbed reactions to the death of a sibling. *American Journal of Orthopsychiatry, 34,* 741-752.

Cairns, N., Clark, G., Smith, S. & Lansky, S. (1979). Adaptation of siblings to childhood malignancy. *The Journal of Pediatrics, 95,* 484-487.

Drotar, D. & Crawford, P. (1985). Psychological adaptation of siblings of chronically ill children: Research and practice implications. *Developmental and Behavioral Pediatrics, 6,* 355-362.

Gogan, J., Koocher, G., Foster, D. & O'Malley, J. (1977). Impact of childhood cancer on siblings. *Health and Social Work, 2,* 41-57.

Kagen-Goodheart, L. (1977). Reentry: Living with childhood cancer. *American Journal of Orthopsychiatry, 47,* 651-658.

Koch, A. (1985). "If only it could be me"; The families of pediatric cancer patients. *Family Relations, 34,* 63-70.

Lavigne, J. & Ryan, M. (1979). Psychological adjustment of siblings of children with chronic illness. *Pediatrics, 63,* 616-627.

Lindsay, M. & MacCarthy, D. (1974). Caring for the brothers and sisters of a dying child. In L. Burton (Ed.), *Care of the child facing death* (pp. 189-206). London and Boston: Routledge and Kegan Paul.

McKeever, P. (1983). Siblings of chronically ill children: A literature review with implications for research and practice. *American Journal of Orthopsychiatry, 53,* 209-218.

Share, L. (1972). Family communication in the crisis of a child's fatal illness: A literature review and analysis. *Omega, 3.*

Sourkes, B. (1977). Facilitating family coping with childhood cancer. *Journal of Pediatric Psychology, 2,* 65-67.

Sourkes, B. (1980). Siblings of the pediatric cancer patient. In J. Kellerman (Ed.), *Psychological aspects of childhood cancer* (pp. 47-69). Springfield, IL: Charles C. Thomas.

Sourkes, B. (1982). *The deepening shade: Psychological aspects of life-threatening illness.* Pittsburgh: University of Pittsburgh Press.

Spinetta, J. J. (1981). The sibling of the child with cancer. In J. J. Spinetta & P. Deasy-Spinetta (Eds.), *Living with childhood cancer* (pp. 133-142). St. Louis: C. V. Mosby.

Townes, B. & Wold, D. (1977). Childhood leukemia. In E. Pattison (Ed.), *The experience of dying* (pp. 133-143). Englewood Cliffs: Prentice-Hall.

Wiener, J. (1970). Reaction of the family to the fatal illness of a child. In B. Schoen-
berg, A. Carr, D. Peretz & A. Kutscher (Eds.), *Loss and grief: Psychological management in medical practice* (pp. 87-101). New York and London: Columbia University Press.

PART III:
CAN SIBLINGS BE
PART OF THE SOLUTION?

Siblings as Teachers and Therapists

Brenda K. Bryant, PhD
Cindy Litman, MS

SUMMARY. Sibling relations at their best encompass both sensitive comforting and conflictual interchanges as do productive therapeutic and educational encounters. To help practitioners see how siblings can function as therapists and teachers, this paper focuses on understanding how sibling helping occurs in natural and research settings. Siblings as teachers and therapists are viewed from two perspectives: first, within the context of the family system, and second, as a distinct dyadic relational system. Both possibilities and limitations of sibling helping are discussed.

Sibling relations at their best encompass both sensitive comforting and conflictual interchanges as do productive therapeutic

Brenda K. Bryant is Professor of Human Development and Family Studies and Cindy Litman is a doctoral graduate student, University of California, Davis, Davis, CA 95616.

Funding for this paper has been provided by the Agriculture Experiment Station, University of California, Davis.

and educational encounters. A simultaneous discussion of siblings participating as teachers and therapists is conceptually satisfying in that both roles entail strategies for problem solving (instrumentality) and modulation of affect (expressiveness). Some sort of balance between nurturance and challenge is necessary for therapeutic or educational progress. In this paper, teaching and therapy will be discussed in the context of sibling support and sibling instrumental challenge or conflict. Reports of sibling relations in natural and research settings will be used to help practitioners formulate how siblings can function as therapists and teachers.

The role of siblings as teachers and therapists will be examined in this paper from two perspectives: first, as part of a larger social system (in this paper the family system), and second, as a distinct dyadic subsystem. Both these views have implications for clinical and educational assessment and intervention involving siblings.

SIBLING RELATIONS AS PART OF A FAMILY SYSTEM

It is of utmost importance to know under what circumstances we can best use siblings as teachers and therapists. While a therapeutic or learning relation may focus on the dyadic interchange between siblings, sibling relations frequently are influenced by the context of a larger group. These influences require our consideration.

Consider in particular the family system. Because parent-parent, parent-child, and child-child relationships operate simultaneously within the family, interactions between any two members of a subsystem can be affected by the behavior of other family members (Cicirelli, 1976). In considering sibling relations then, it is useful to consider the ways in which family members outside the sibling subsystem affect sibling relations in general and explore the implication of such indirect effects for siblings helping siblings. Three such indirect effects will be examined: (a) the impact of parental availability/unavailability on the sibling relationship; (b) the impact of differential treatment of one sibling over another; and (c) the impact on one sibling of the combined behavior of another sibling plus a parent.

The Impact of Parental Availability/Unavailability on Sibling Relations

Studies covering a wide range of ages suggest that maternal psychological and physical unavailability stimulates interactive, prosocial behavior between siblings by creating the opportunity for older children to engage more actively in helping a younger child and by encouraging the younger child to use an older sibling as a resource (Bryant & Crockenberg, 1980; Corter, Abramovitch & Pepler, 1983; Dunn & Kendrick, 1982; Samuels, 1980; Stewart, 1983). In this paper, we will define parental unavailability as follows: (a) physically distant, (b) physically absent, (c) physically and/or mentally ill, and (d) interpersonally conflictual and combative with child (in research it has been maternal unavailability that has been most closely monitored). Under all these forms of parental distancing, sibling bonds are generally enhanced.

The very presence of mothers has been found to reduce sibling interaction, particularly prosocial behavior (Corter et al., 1983). When mothers are absent or physically distant, older siblings in particular appear to comfort their younger counterpart and younger siblings seek out older available siblings. Stewart (1983) studied the responses of preschool children to their younger siblings' distress at being separated from their mothers. More than half of the older siblings in the study responded to the distress of a younger sibling with some form of therapeutic response (i.e., approaching or hugging the infant). Under more stressful conditions such as the entrance of a strange adult when the mother was still absent, younger siblings approached and sought reassurance from older siblings, whether brothers or sisters. Samuels (1980) found that when mothers were instructed to be physically distant (remain seated at the periphery of an unfamiliar backyard) and instructed to be responsive but refrain from directing the actions of their children, children benefited from having older siblings present. When an older sibling was present, infants left their mothers sooner, inspected features of the environment more, displayed less distress, and were more independent (often following the sibling to some location in the yard and then remaining to explore after the older sibling moved on). In other words, in the absence (absolute or relative) of their mothers, older siblings offered and younger siblings requested and/or accepted a therapeutic alliance. The benefits of this alliance for the younger sibling include less distress and greater orientation toward learning through exploration.

With respect to psychological unavailability, Dunn and Kendrick (1982) found that when mothers were very tired or depressed following the birth of their second-born children, the two siblings had a particularly friendly relationship 14 months later. Results from this study also documented that in families where mothers and older daughters engaged in frequent confrontations at the time of the younger sibling's birth, sibling relations were especially friendly when the younger child was 14 months old. Similarly, Bryant and Crockenberg (1980) found that when mothers frequently ignored requests for help from their school-aged daughters, older daughters displayed increased prosocial involvement with their younger sisters. Younger sisters, in turn, were more willing to accept help from older sisters under this condition. These data suggest that siblings may be a particularly valuable resource for those children whose parents (due to either personal or interpersonal problems) are limited in their ability to meet their child's needs. At least this appears to hold true for younger siblings.

A word of caution is warranted. These findings should not be interpreted to mean that parental unavailability solely benefits sibling relations. Sibling abuse is far more common than is typically recognized (Brenner, 1984). Based on injuries that would warrant a charge of child abuse against a parent, Straus, Gelles, and Steinmetz (1980) found in their nationally representative study of family violence that severe sibling abuse occurred in more than half of the families they studied over the course of a year, and parental lack of supervision or intervention has been implicated in this phenomenon (Bank & Kahn, 1982; Tooley, 1977). Bryant and Crockenberg (1980) also found that maternal unavailability in response to requests for help was associated with increased conflictual or antisocial interchanges between siblings. Thus, while parental unavailability may promote enhanced sibling bonding, this bonding is not always beneficial and warrants adult watchfulness.

Implications for Application

1. As part of a family assessment, it is relevant to determine whether or not a younger sibling will seek an older sibling for comfort and, similarly, whether or not an older sibling will offer reassurance to a younger sibling in distress.

2. For a thorough sibling assessment, careful analysis of siblings under varying forms of separation, physical as well as psychological, from the parents is necessary. Interviewing and observing siblings alone without parents is not part of our tradition in child or family therapy, but research indicates that such an approach is warranted if we are to fully assess the potential for siblings to participate as teachers and therapists.

3. When developing a family intervention strategy, assess and consider the degree to which parents are able to distance themselves from their children. To allow a productive sibling relationship to develop, parents may need to distance themselves from sibling interaction.

4. Social workers, medical personnel, judicial officers, and others with decision-making power over children are cautioned against unnecessary separation of siblings, particularly in times of family stress. For example, hospital personnel frequently ban sibling visits, even though siblings may help children gain interest in exploring the environment, a factor which may speed the child's recovery. In the school setting, children who move to a new school may benefit from being accompanied to their new classroom by an older sibling. In the judicial context, child custody decisions should be sensitive to the value of one sibling offering comfort to another before recommending separation of siblings. This seems particularly important during the early years following divorce when parents are generally less able to meet their children's needs (Hetherington & Camara, 1984). These three examples illustrate how siblings can be used as therapists and teachers in times of stress.

5. When a sibling dyad is strongly bonded, consideration needs to be given as to whether the older sibling's needs are being met. In adopting caretaking roles in a family, there is the risk that the child's own wants and feelings may be overlooked or denied (Brenner, 1984).

6. Certain child characteristics foster the use of siblings as therapists or teachers. If a younger child is particularly timid, the aid of an older sibling may be particularly useful to consider.

7. Finally, if an extremely strong sibling bond is observed at school or elsewhere, attention is warranted to determine whether or not this sibling alliance reflects some sort of serious parental neglect (unavailability) at home. Strong sibling bonding can be beneficial, but it can also be the context for physical (including sexual) and emotional sibling abuse. This needs to be recognized and assessed for what it is.

The Impact of the Differential Treatment of One Sibling Over Another

Historically, psychological theory has focused on differential treatment of siblings as a major source of sibling personality development. For purposes of thinking about siblings as teachers and therapists, parental as well as other significant persons' differential treatment of siblings can interfere with the establishment of a comfortable sibling relationship and with adjustment in the home and school environment (Bryant & Crockenberg, 1980; Daniels, Dunn, Furstenberg & Plomin, 1985; Pfouts, 1976).

Where parental treatment of siblings differs (i.e., one sibling experiences greater maternal closeness or greater say in family decision-making), corresponding differences in children's adjustment have been found, and this is true for both parental or sibling reports of differential treatment (Daniels et al., 1985). Research indicates it is not simply an effect of interaction with parents, but it indicates that the sibling relationship is impaired when differential treatment is experienced. In an observational study of school-age sisters and their mothers, Bryant and Crockenberg (1980) found that when one child had expressed needs met to a high degree while the other sibling in the pair did not, sibling discomforting of each other was high. In other words, it appears that if a child's expressed needs are not met, relative to another sibling, the child antagonizes the sibling who responds in kind.

Finally, school and community sources can be the basis for social comparison and sibling rivalry or discomfort. Pfouts

(1976) found that when brothers in middle-class, two-boy families differed significantly in culturally valued personality or intellectual assets, the child who suffered from the comparison experienced resentment and ill will toward the brother who outshone him. In addition, the more able child in the pair was not resentful of the less able sibling but did report feelings of discomfort and ambivalence in the sibling relationship. The possibility of siblings utilizing one another as a teacher or therapist is reduced when differential regard is given to the two siblings at home or in the community at large.

We can infer that children are likely to compare the extent of attention they get from a parent or significant other with what another sibling gets. Furthermore, ill will is characteristic of both siblings, not just the child who gets the short end of the parental resources. We can probably safely say that differential treatment of siblings does not remedy any existing sibling difficulty but rather exacerbates, if not creates, it.

Implications for Application

1. Differential treatment of siblings by parents and other significant others (e.g., teachers) appears to disturb the development of satisfying sibling relationships. When siblings cannot make use of one another for comfort and help, an assessment of siblings' experience of differential treatment by significant adults is particularly warranted.

2. Three basic approaches to assessing differential or equal treatment of siblings have been used. The first approach calls for asking the siblings themselves. A second method involves observing the amount of interaction or attention given each sibling by a third person. The third method notes how often children's expressed needs are actually met. This last method makes it possible to evaluate the extent to which the siblings are equally demanding as well as the extent to which the parents are responding to their needs unequally. All three methods are available to the practitioner and provide the basis for relevant intervention strategies.

The Combined Impact of Sibling and Parent
on Another Sibling

A family systems approach provides a view of the family as an interdependent organization in which the behavior of each family member influences and is influenced by all others. The combined impact of two or more family members acting on another can differ from their impact when acting singly. Thus, a sibling and a parent acting together can influence another sibling. In the one available study that systematically documents the effectiveness of a sibling as a therapeutic agent, Lavigueur (1976) found that the combined therapeutic efforts of siblings and parents were helpful in modifying a child's disruptive behavior when both parent and sibling had encouraged the disruptive behavior in the first place.

Among normal (nonclinic) children, Bryant (in press – a,b) illustrates the combined impact of older siblings and parents on the development of social skills in younger siblings. For example, firm limit setting by mother (e.g., with respect to misbehavior at home or school) seems to enhance the younger siblings ability to take the perspective of another (i.e., to understand the feelings and motives of others). If, however, an older sister is intrusive (whether she is punitive or nurturant), then the limit-setting by the mother may not have the desired effect. Thus, the impact of the parent's teaching strategy on the younger sibling is affected by the behavior of the older sibling.

Bryant (in press – b) further suggests that a double dose of either nurturance or punishment from both a parent and an older sibling can be counterproductive for the development of peer relations in the younger sibling. Bryant found that sibling nurturance and supportive challenge when combined with parental concern or support appears to interfere with children's accepting a variety of peers into their lives. At the same time, sibling punishment combined with paternal punishment was also found to be associated with the younger sibling's diminished acceptance of individual differences among peers. The double dose of sibling plus parent nurturance mimic what Minuchin (1974) calls the enmeshed family in which family member are too close. In contrast, the double dose of punishment mimics Minuchin's (1974) disengaged family, with members too distant from one another. In either case, the double dose of either nurturance or punishment appears to interfere with the development of peer relations in the younger sibling.

Not all combinations of sibling and parent caregiving strategies are counterproductive for the younger sibling. On the contrary, parents and siblings can coordinate their efforts for the benefit of the younger sibling. For example, in their cross-cultural work, Weisner and Gallimore (1977) found that when older siblings assumed some routine responsibility for the care of younger siblings, parents were free to engage in more positive interactions and activities with children. This suggests that older siblings might provide an important resource for families in which parents are particularly stressed by parental responsibilities, by indirectly affecting children's relationships with their parents.

Implications for Application

1. What may appear to be the influence of a parent or a sibling acting alone, may actually be the influence of a coordinated system of caretaking among siblings and parents. The impact of an older sibling's support, challenge, or punishment on a younger sibling often depends on the behavior of the parents, and the parents' impact can also depend on a sibling's behavior. For example, a double dose of either punishment (from a father and an older sibling) or nurturance (from a mother and an older sibling) may interfere with the younger sibling's relations with peers.

2. Therapeutic efforts may need to include parents and siblings to solve problem behaviors in another sibling, especially when parents and siblings contributed to the problem in the first place.

3. Siblings may be indirect caregiving agents by providing parents with help in household care and maintenance (including care of other siblings) which can leave the parent(s) with time and energy to work with a sibling who is having personal or academic problems. This strategy must be used with care to avoid problems which result from differential treatment of siblings by parents.

THE SIBLING DYAD

Although siblings operate as part of a family system, it is useful to consider the siblings as a dyad in its own right. Children seek out older siblings for frequent dyadic interchange, and cross-cultural research has shown that older children (frequently siblings) respond positively to the bids for help from younger children (Whiting, 1982). In the United States, siblings often help with homework. One study showed that 78% of later-born children report that they have a sibling who, when asked, helped them with their homework (Bryant, 1982). This was true for first graders and fourth graders, males and females, children from small families and large families, and whether the older sibling was a brother or a sister. The nature of sibling involvement, however, is much more comprehensive than simple direct caretaking or tutoring.

Pfouts (1976) has argued that because sibling relationships are so firmly rooted in ambivalence, they are more likely to be stressful and volatile than most other human relationships; love and hate are seen as the two sides of the sibling coin. On the one side is sibling rivalry. On the other side is psychological closeness, supportive caretaking, direct instruction, and facilitative modeling of developmental milestones.

To more carefully examine the sibling dyad relation, let us look at how sibling interactions differ from child-adult interactions and how the relative age of a child in the sibling dyad affects the sibling interaction. Then let us consider the actual skill that siblings bring to a therapist or teacher role during childhood.

Sibling Interactions in Comparison to Child-Adult Interactions

Children's interactions with others are clearly affected by the relative age status of the other person. Behavior toward adults is based on the child's dependency and the adult's need to control while child-child interactions are characterized by greater equality (Hartup, 1983). Cross-cultural research, reported by Whiting and Whiting (1975) and generally supported by family research in the United States (Baskett & Johnson, 1982; Furman & Buhrmester, 1985), has provided a picture of the following differences between adult-child and child-child social systems (with much child-child social interaction involving siblings). Dependency and nurturance occurs more frequently in interactions with adults than with peers, whereas, aggression and, in some circumstances, sociable behaviors are more commonly observed in peer interactions than in adult-child relations.

The research is most consistent in finding conflict to be a salient feature of sibling interactions in contrast to interactions with adults (Baskett & Johnson, 1982; Bryant, in press-b; Furman & Buhrmester, 1985; Whiting and Whiting, 1975). With respect to therapeutic strategies involving siblings, the durability of the sibling relationship (during childhood one can not say "I won't be your sibling" or "I'm never going to speak to you again" and follow through), as well as its aggressive quality suggests that siblings may provide an important, relatively enduring context in which successful control of aggression modulation develops. The lesson that the expression of anger need not threaten mutual attachment and the continuity of relations may be one well suited for the sibling dyad. The goal of successful aggression modulation is not to eliminate aggression, per se, but rather for children to discriminate when and what kind of aggressive behaviors are appropriate. Consistent with this formulation, Baskett and Johnson (1982) have suggested that siblings might be more appropriate treatment agents than parents for teaching aggressive children to achieve a more normal balance of prosocial and coercive behaviors.

Implications for Application

1. Conflict resolution skills may more easily be developed in sibling interaction than in parent-child interaction. Professionals may find it useful to work with siblings without the parents present so that issues of conflict can be considered without being clouded by parent-child issues.

2. Similarly, companionship skills learned in the sibling interaction rather than in parent-child interaction may more readily generalize to peer relations.

3. Again, while sibling conflict may be useful to a child's

development, physical and emotional abuse is not. Professionals as well as parents must differentiate between healthy sibling conflict and sibling abuse. As Schachter and Stone note (this volume), healthy sibling conflict is less intense, less frequent, and relatively short-lived. Schachter and Stone also recommended protecting siblings by prohibiting the use of physical objects in sibling conflict.

Younger and Older Siblings in Interaction (Relative Age)

One of the most consistent findings from studies of sibling interaction is that the contribution made by each child to the sibling interaction is greatly influenced by whether the child is relatively older or younger. In reviewing the research, one obtains a clear picture of role complementarity with the older child more frequently initiating and controlling the interaction and the younger child more frequently accepting control. This asymmetry in sibling interactions remains remarkably consistent throughout childhood.

Older children initiate both more prosocial and more antagonistic behavior than younger siblings (Abramovitch, Corter, Pepler & Stanhope, 1986; Berndt & Bulleit, 1985), and these differences are not trivial. In comparison to younger siblings aged three to five, their older siblings initiated two times as much prosocial behavior, most notably in the areas of cooperation, helping, comforting, and praising (Abramovitch et al., 1986; Pepler, Abramovitch & Corter, 1981). These older siblings also initiated twice as much antagonistic behavior. Older siblings are also more frequent providers of instrumental aid (Furman & Buhrmester, 1985), assuming the role of teacher, manager, and helper (Brody, Stoneman & MacKinnon, 1982; Brody, Stoneman, MacKinnon & MacKinnon, 1985; Stoneman, Brody & MacKinnon, 1984). Overall, the behavior of older siblings may serve to make them an especially salient feature in the lives of their younger siblings. Baskett (1984) found that younger siblings were more likely to attend to the behavior of an older sibling than to the behavior of a parent.

While the relatively older siblings appear to initiate interaction more often than do younger siblings, the younger siblings appear to have an important role in maintaining the interaction by reciprocating positively to prosocial behavior, submitting to aggressive behavior, and imitating their siblings (Pepler et al., 1981). Furthermore, younger siblings attend more to their older siblings than vice-versa, monitoring their activities, imitating them, and accepting objects abandoned or offered by them (Baskett, 1984; Brody et al., 1985; Pepler et al., 1981; Lamb, 1978a,b). In addition, younger siblings respond more positively to the prosocial behavior of their older siblings (Abramovitch et al., 1986; Pepler et al., 1981) and accept their management and help (Brody et al., 1985) more frequently than do older siblings.

Aggressive acts initiated by older siblings are also more passively accepted by younger siblings. Younger siblings most frequently submit to the aggression of older siblings, while older siblings are more likely to counterattack (Abramovitch et al., 1986). Finally, younger siblings are more self-deprecating in sibling interactions than are older siblings (Minnett, Vandell & Santrock, 1983).

Altogether, older siblings behave like the dominant, powerful member of the dyad, younger siblings like the powerless one, as might be expected from the real disparities in their power (i.e., in their physical prowess and their intellectual competence). Do these complementary roles in sibling interaction generalize to interactions with other people? Do they result in consistent personality differences between younger and older siblings? Are firstborns generally more dominant and later-borns more submissive? The evidence suggests that the answer to these questions is "no." For example, Abramovitch et al. (1986) found that the complementary roles of older and younger siblings do not generalize to their relationships with peers. In fact, younger siblings assume the dominant role when they are in a position of power, as when a peer is visiting their home.

Some investigators suggest that the experience of teaching a younger child is beneficial for social-emotional as well as intellectual development. The benefits cited include having a better attitude toward school and teachers, becoming more responsible, and thinking more highly of oneself (Allen & Feldman, 1976) as well as attaining a higher IQ score (Zajonc & Marcus, 1975). Older children who assume responsibility for younger children

(often their own siblings) have also been found to be more prosocial than children who lack such experience (Whiting & Whiting,
1975).

Other investigators (Scarr & Grajek, 1982; Falbo, 1982) have
raised questions about these conclusions. For example, Falbo
(1982) questions whether only children are disadvantaged by not
having a younger sibling to teach. Until further evidence resolves
this controversy concerning the benefits of teaching a younger
child, it should be noted that this teaching experience is available
to all children whether the young child is a sibling or not.

Implications for Application

1. Practitioners and parents who are appalled by older siblings'
domination of younger siblings can be reassured that this is a
commonplace phenomenon, probably based on the power differential between the children. They can also be reassured that the
dominant role of the older sibling and the submissive role of the
younger one does not characteristically generalize to other social
and personal situations. The younger sibling can be dominant
when he/she is in a position of power. Assessment of a given
child in various kinds of relationships is probably the best basis
for resolving a concern in this matter.

2. Until further evidence is available to the contrary, the opportunity to teach younger siblings may be viewed as enhancing
the child's sense of responsibility and expectations about his/her
own competencies. Younger siblings could perhaps be provided
with opportunities to teach children younger than themselves so
that they too can reap the benefits of the experience of teaching.

Actual Skill of Siblings as Teachers or Therapists

Differences in the characteristics of the parent-child and sibling subsystems noted above suggest that the quality of academic
and affective caregiving received from a sibling differs from that
received from a parent. Based on cross-cultural studies, Weisner
and Gallimore (1977) note that whether or not a sibling caretaker
is trying consciously to imitate the parents, the child's need to
balance the simultaneous demands of parents and the small

charges as well as the child caretaker's greater immaturity conspire to make caretaking delivered by a child very different from parental care.

Skills of Siblings as Teachers

Consistent with these cross-cultural observations, Bryant and Crockenberg (1980) found few similarities between the behavior of mothers and older siblings when an older sibling (fourth- or fifth-grade sister) was assigned the role of helper to her younger sister, even on a task in which the mother had just previously played that role to the two girls herself. At least in middle childhood, girls do not appear to adopt the teaching/helping strategies employed by their mothers when they act as helper to a younger sister. For example, the more the mother offered unsolicited help, encouragement, and approval, the more the older sibling offered unsolicited disapproval. This suggests that the older sibling may have attempted to forcefully help and encourage, but her behavior more closely resembled negative help and negative encouragement. It appears, then, that female siblings in middle childhood lack the skills, but not necessarily the intent of their mothers in caretaking endeavors.

Sisters, nonetheless, appear to be more apt, formal and deductive teachers to their younger siblings than are older brothers. Cicirelli (1972) found that girls teaching their siblings tended to use the deductive method (i.e., the student is to infer particulars from general principles) more often than did boys. Boys, on the other hand, tended to use the inductive method (i.e., the student is required to conclude general principles from particulars) to teach their siblings. Sisters may be most appropriate when deductive teaching is desired but brothers may be more desirable teachers when the teaching process called upon is inductive.

Not only do older siblings vary in their teaching styles, younger siblings respond differently to an older brother or sister who teaches them. Cicirelli (1974) found that children were more likely to accept nonverbal direction from a sister than from a brother. Cicirelli (1973) also found that younger siblings were more likely to work independently of an older brother than of an older sister, further suggesting that younger siblings are more willing to accept an older sister in the role of formal teacher. In formal, deductive teaching, then, the younger school-aged child is thought to learn more from an older sister than from an older brother (Cicirelli, 1975). Where independent thinking is the aim of an academic exercise, however, brothers may be desirable teachers.

Educational and cultural background should also be considered in discussing sibling teaching skills. In a study of Israeli children of Asian and African descent, older siblings assumed teaching roles with younger siblings in large families with poorly educated parents (Cicirelli, 1978). In these families, where the academic competence of older siblings surpasses that of the parents, sibling teaching can be particularly beneficial. Other cultural factors may operate to make sibling tutoring an especially valuable experience. In cultures which emphasize sibling interdependence, this appears to be the case. Weisner and Gallimore (1977) reported that siblings were an especially valuable component of an Hawaiian school program where children came from homes characterized by close sibling interdependence. It can be seen that cultural and educational backgrounds of family members can affect the value of employing siblings as teachers and helpers of younger siblings.

Skills of Siblings as Therapists

There is virtually no systematic data available on this issue. Clinical reports suggest that siblings can play the useful role of offering negative evaluations to the identified child client. Greenbaum (1965) reports that sibling evaluations of one another are more readily tolerated than the same evaluations offered by an adult.

Our own cursory review of taped discussions of younger siblings confiding to older siblings about worried, sad, and angry experiences indicates that siblings in middle childhood and early adolescence are, by and large, not very skilled at providing either comforting or problem solving strategies. Nonetheless, there was a great range of skill in both domains demonstrated across the 168 sibling pairs studied.

To illustrate this wide range of skills, we close with the following two vignettes, the first showing a sibling completely lacking in therapeutic and teaching skills, the second showing a sibling who tries to help in a variety of ways. Both vignettes involve two sisters; the younger sisters are age 10, and the older sisters are age 12 or 13. Both younger sisters are talking to their older sisters about worry, anger, and other painful experiences.

VIGNETTE #1

Older sibling: Wait! Stop jabbering, jabbermouth!

Younger sibling: I was worried when Mom was having a Mary Kay cosmetic party, remember?

Older sibling: Oh, yeah.

Younger sibling: And you guys — Dad was going in the living room and then got mad at you guys and I hyperventilated.

Older sibling: That's all you ever do. You're so dumb.

Younger sibling: And you had to take me to the hospital. I was two hours out there. That was the time I was 6 years old.

Older sibling: You weren't 6. Five and a half.

Younger sibling: I wasn't five and a half. I was in second grade.

Older sibling: No, you weren't. I am sorry about that but.

Younger sibling: I wasn't in kindergarten.

Older sibling: But you were in kindergarten.

Younger sibling: Then I was hyperventilating for five years.

Older sibling: Bull!

Younger sibling: I couldn't breathe.

Older sibling: No, duh.

Younger sibling: O.K. I went to the doctor before because I had bronchitis and the doctor said I'd be just fine — just give me some ice or something.

Older sibling: He was a dumbbell.

Younger sibling: Alright. And my throat was all swollen. It was swollen shut.

Older sibling: It was swollen open!

Younger sibling: I forgot to — you know a little kindergartner — couldn't breathe — they take their time sticking a thermometer in your mouth.

Older sibling: Then I was worried too. Worried that you might live.

VIGNETTE #2

Younger sibling: I was angry when I didn't get my drums for Christmas or for my birthday. 'Cause Mom said that they would be too noisy and that we wouldn't have anywhere to put them. So I wouldn't get them.

Older sibling: Well, maybe Dad had to work or something. He has to have room.

Younger sibling: I know. But I could put them out in the garage.

Older sibling: There's no room.

Younger sibling: I know.

Older sibling: You, you could, maybe make room if you cleared out the garage.

Younger sibling: No thanks.

Implications for Application

1. Older sisters may be more able than brothers to teach formal, deductive lessons. Older brothers, on the other hand, may be a more appropriate choice for lessons involving an inductive and independent-thinking approach.
2. Children from families in which parents lack an adequate education may benefit most directly from tutoring by older, educated siblings.
3. Children from cultures which emphasize sibling interdependence are likely to find sibling tutoring projects especially beneficial as they are accustomed to relying on siblings.
4. While children may often lack the teaching skills of adults, their acceptance by individual siblings may make up for the lack of skill.
5. There is a wide range of caregiving skills among siblings so that it becomes important to assess these skills before assigning a sibling to a teaching or therapeutic role.

Finally, there is the lesson to be learned from the "No thanks" of the younger sister in our second vignette, as she rejects the advice of her older sister. The elder can advise, but the younger need not consent. No doubt, children find it easier to reject instruction from siblings than from parents, given the respect for (and fear of) adult authority. Does this mean that siblings, even when their skills equal adults', are bound to be less effective as teachers? Not necessarily. In fact, our major theory of intellectual development, that of the late Jean Piaget (1973), holds that children learn more from the free exchange of ideas among equals than from docile submission to adult authority. If so, then we can conclude that in the give and take of sibling relationships, in their endless arguments and debates, in the challenging clash of conflicting ideas and beliefs, siblings are likely to learn a great deal from each other.

REFERENCES

Abramovitch, R., Corter, C., Pepler, D. & Stanhope, L. (1986). Sibling and peer interaction. A final follow-up and a comparison. *Child Development, 57,* 217-229.

Allen, V. L. & Feldman, R. S. (1976). Studies on the role of tutor. In V. L. Allen (Ed.), *Children as teachers: Theory and research on tutoring.* N.Y.: Academic Press.

Bank, S. & Kahn, M. D. (1982). Intense sibling loyalties. In M. E. Lamb & B. Sutton-Smith (Eds.), *Sibling relationships: Their nature and significance across the lifespan.* Hillsdale, N.J.: Erlbaum.

Baskett, L. M. (1984). Ordinal position differences in children's family interactions. *Developmental Psychology, 20,* 1026-1031.

Baskett, L. M. & Johnson, S. M. (1982). The young child's interactions with parents versus siblings: A behavioral analysis. *Child Development, 53,* 643-650.

Berndt, T. J. & Bulleit, T. N. (1985). Effects of sibling relationships on preschoolers' behavior at home and at school. *Developmental Psychology, 21,* 761-767.

Brenner, A. (1984). *Helping children cope with stress.* Lexington, Mass.: D. Heath and Company.

Brody, G. H., Stoneman, Z. & MacKinnon, C. E. (1982). Role asymmetries in interactions among school-aged children, their young siblings, and their friends. *Child Development, 53,* 1364-1370.

Brody, G. H., Stoneman, Z., MacKinnon, C. E. & MacKinnon, R. (1985). Role relationships and behavior between preschool-aged and school-aged sibling pairs. *Developmental Psychology, 21,* 124-129.

Bryant, B. K. (in press – a). Mental health, temperament, family, and friends: Perspectives on children's empathy and social perspective taking. In N. Eisenberg & J. Strayer (Eds.), *Empathy and its development.* New York: Cambridge University Press.

Bryant, B. K. (in press – b). The child's perspective of sibling caretaking and its relevance to understanding social-emotional functioning and development. In P. Zukow (Ed.), *Sibling interaction across cultures.* New York: Springer-Verlag.

Bryant, B. K. (1982). Sibling relationships in middle childhood. In M. E. Lamb & B. Sutton-Smith (Eds.), *Sibling relationships: Their nature and significance across the lifespan.* Hillsdale, N.J.: Erlbaum.

Bryant, B. K. & Crockenberg, S. B. (1980). Correlates and dimensions of prosocial behavior: A study of female siblings with their mothers. *Child Development, 51,* 529-544.

Cicirelli, V. G. (1972). The effect of sibling relationships on concept learning of young children taught by child-teachers. *Child Development, 43*, 282-287.

Cicirelli, V. G. (1973). Effects of sibling structure and interaction on children's categorization style. *Developmental Psychology, 9*, 132-139.

Cicirelli, V. G. (1974). Relationship of sibling structure and interaction to younger sib's conceptual style. *The Journal of Genetic Psychology, 125*, 37-49.

Cicirelli, V. G. (1975). Effects of mother and older sibling on the problem-solving behavior of the younger child. *Developmental Psychology, 11*, 749-756.

Cicirelli, V. G. (1976). Mother-child and sibling-sibling interactions on a problem-solving task. *Child Development, 47*, 588-596.

Cicirelli, V. G. (1978). The relationship of sibling structure to intellectual abilities and achievement. *Review of Educational Research, 48*, 365-379.

Corter, C., Abramovitch, R. & Pepler, D. J. (1983). The role of the mother in sibling interaction. *Child Development, 54*, 1599-1605.

Daniels, D., Dunn, J. Furstenberg, F. F. & Plomin, R. (1985). Environmental differences within the family and adjustment differences within pairs of adolescent siblings. *Child Development, 56*, 764-774.

Dunn, J. & Kendrick, C. (1982). Siblings and their mothers: Developing relationships within the family. In M. E. Lamb & B. Sutton-Smith (Eds.), *Sibling relationships: Their nature and significance across the lifespan.* Hillsdale, N.J.: Erlbaum.

Falbo, T. (1982). Only children in America. In M. E. Lamb & B. Sutton-Smith (Eds.), *Sibling relationships: Their nature and significance across the lifespan.* Hillsdale, N.J.: Erlbaum.

Furman, W. & Buhrmester, D. (1985). Children's perceptions of the personal relationships in their social networks. *Developmental Psychology, 21*, 1016-1024.

Greenbaum, M. (1965). Joint sibling interview as a diagnostic procedure. *Journal of Child Psychology and Psychiatry, 6*, 227-232.

Hartup, W. W. (1983). Peer relations. In P. H. Mussen (Ed.), *The handbook of child psychology: Vol. 4. Socialization, personality, and social development.* New York: Wiley.

Hetherington, E. M. & Camara, K. A. (1984). Families in transition. The processes of dissolution and reconstitution. In R. D. Parke (Ed.), *The family: Review of child development research* (Vol. 7). Chicago: University of Chicago Press.

Lamb, M. E. (1978a). Interactions between eighteen-month-olds and their preschool-aged siblings. *Child Development, 49*, 51-59.

Lamb, M. E. (1978b). The development of sibling relationships in infancy: A short-term longitudinal study. *Child Development, 49*, 1189-1196.

Lavigueur, H. (1976). The use of siblings as an adjunct to the behavioral treatment of children in the home with parents as therapists. *Behavior Therapy, 7*, 602-613.

Minnett, A. M., Vandell, D. L. & Santrock, J. W. (1983). The effects of sibling status on sibling interaction: Influence of birth order, age spacing, sex of child, and sex of sibling. *Child Development, 54*, 1064-1072.

Minuchin, S. (1974). *Families and family therapy.* Cambridge, Mass.: Harvard University Press.

Pepler, D., Abramovitch, R. & Corter, C. (1981). Sibling interaction in the home: A longitudinal study. *Child Development, 52*, 1344-1347.

Pfouts, J. H. (1976). The sibling relationship: A forgotten dimension. *Social Work, 21*, 200-204.

Piaget, J. (1973). *The child and reality.* New York: Grossman.

Samuels, H. R. (1980). The effect of an older sibling on infant locomotor exploration of a new environment. *Child Development, 51*, 607-609.

Scarr, S. & Grajek, S. (1982). Similarities and differences among siblings. In M. E. Lamb & B. Sutton-Smith (Eds.), *Sibling relationships: Their nature and significance across the lifespan*. Hillsdale, N.J.: Erlbaum.

Stewart, R. B. (1983). Sibling attachment relationships: Child-infant interactions in the strange situation. *Developmental Psychology, 19*, 192-199.

Stoneman, Z., Brody, G. H. & MacKinnon, C. (1984). Naturalistic observations of children's activities and roles while playing with their siblings and friends. *Child Development, 55*, 617-627.

Straus, M. A., Gelles, R. J. & Steinmetz, S. K. (1980). *Behind closed doors: Violence in the American family*. Garden City, N.Y.: Anchor Books, Doubleday.

Tooley, K. M. (1977). The young child as victim of sibling attack. *Social Casework, 58*, 25-28.

Weisner, T. & Gallimore, R. (1977). My brother's keeper: Child and sibling caretaking. *Current Anthropology, 18*, 169-190.

Whiting, B. B. (1982). The genesis of prosocial behavior. In D. Bridgeman (Ed.), *The nature of prosocial development*. New York: Academic Press.

Whiting, B. B. & Whiting, J. W. M. (1975). *Children of six cultures: A psycho-cultural analysis*. Cambridge, Mass.: Harvard University Press.

Zajonc, R. B. & Markus, G. B. (1975). Birth order and intellectual development. *Psychological Review, 31*, 141-162.

Subject Index